The Way

of the

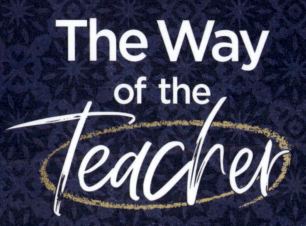

Teacher

40 principles for
success in the
classroom and life

New York Times Bestselling Author
Dr. Kevin Leman and
Kristin Leman O'Reilly

BroadStreet
PUBLISHING

BroadStreet Publishing ® Group, LLC
Savage, Minnesota, USA
BroadStreetPublishing.com

*The Way of the Teacher: 40 Principles for Success
in the Classroom and Life*
Copyright © 2025 KAL Enterprises, Inc. & Kristin Leman O'Reilly

9781424569090 (faux)
9781424569106 (ebook)

Editors: Ramona Cramer Tucker, Michelle Winger

To protect the privacy of those who have shared their stories with the authors, details and names have been changed.

Stock or custom editions of BroadStreet Publishing titles may be purchased in bulk for educational, business, ministry, fundraising, or sales promotional use. For information, please email orders@ broadstreetpublishing.com.

Cover and interior by Garborg Design Works| garborgdesign.com

Printed in China

25 26 27 28 29 5 4 3 2 1

To my precious teacher,
Ms. Eleanor Wilson,
whose insight and challenging wisdom
enabled me to turn my life
in a positive direction.
DR. KEVIN LEMAN

To my Mom and Dad,
who have been by my side, encouraging
and supporting me in everything I do.
Your unconditional love and devotion
to our family have impacted my life greatly.
I love you forever.
Thank you for always believing in me.
KRISTIN LEMAN O'REILLY

CONTENTS

INTRODUCTION

Learning is a lifelong process of keeping abreast of change.
And the most pressing task is to teach people how to learn.
PETER DRUCKER

We applaud you, Teacher. You are among the ranks of those most capable of changing the world in beneficial ways. William Ayres once said, "Teaching is the vocation of vocations," and he's right. No single career has more potential to train and empower individuals for every workplace, home, and community at large. What an unparalleled legacy!

Great teachers introduce knowledge and expand their students' ability to think. They broaden skills by providing questions and prompting discovery. They seek to know and understand each student in order to uniquely motivate, intrigue, and inspire. They role-model responsibility, accountability, respect, and care for others.

Such work is complex. It requires viewing members of each year's class as single lifelong learners within a community and experimenting with the best techniques to reach each child. Add to that never-ending tasks and long hours, especially for fledgling teachers who are stretching their wings, and it's no wonder your energy is flagging by dinnertime.

But let us tell you from firsthand experience, there's no career more rewarding, whether now or down the road. Think for a minute about some of your heart-warming successes.

What about that hug from the kindergartener who was terrified to enter your classroom a week ago? Or the "aha" on the face of the struggling second-grader who finally understood a math problem? What about the "outsider" third-grader who was befriended on the first day by three other classmates? When you thanked them for their kindness to a fellow student, they told you, "Mr. J., we remember what you said about what it's like to not know anybody in class."

Or the uncoordinated sixth-grader who, because of your encouraging words, laughed when she missed catching the ball instead of feigning sickness every PE class? Or the high school junior who punched the classroom wall due to all the pressure he was under to pick the "right" college but was finally able to tell his father how he felt? You still have the thank-you note from his parents for your role in opening their eyes and hearts to their son's needs.

These are only a few of the precious moments you've been a part of while teaching students how to learn. This little book, *The Way of the Teacher*, is designed to support and encourage you in that journey. To start off your exploration, take the "What Kind of Teacher Are You?" quiz (pp. 9-13). Then peek at "What You Need Most" (pp. 177-185) for affirmation and confirmation of your own thoughts.

Our practical wisdom is divided into four sections: A Teacher's Mindset, Classroom Strategies, Student Relations, and Goals and Perspective. Each of the 40 principles leads with an inspiring quote you'll want to post, information to use in practice and to expand your perspective, and concludes with "Classroom Corner" reflection and "Teacher's Toolbelt" tips. The book closes with "The Final Word" encouragement (p. 186) and what your students want you to know in "A Student's 10 Commandments to Teachers" (p. 187).

So go ahead. Change the world one student a time. We double-dare you, because we know you can do it.

WHAT KIND OF TEACHER ARE YOU?

Take This Quick Quiz

TEACHER #1

* You are new to the field, learning the ropes, or still struggle with some teaching basics.

* The simultaneous tasks teachers have to do are so overwhelming. How can you ever catch up, when there's so little of you to go around and so much to do?

* You feel discouraged, wondering if you lack talent and you should be doing something else, or you simply lack support and training.

* You often back down in front of more dominant people, such as parents, grandparents, or administrators.

* New ideas are welcome, but you don't have time to seek them out yourself.

* Other teachers seem to be smarter, better trained, or produce better results than you. Why are you the only one who seems to be struggling?

* You internalize poor results on standardized tests as failure on your part. If students don't learn to their best potential, you assume it's because of your lack of ability and lack in mastering teaching skills.

* You're weighed down by daily requests and wonder if there's a better way to manage them.

If this sounds the most like you, flip to pages 177-178 to see what you need most.

TEACHER #2

* What others think about you as a teacher and your teaching style really matters to you.

* Rainclouds hang over you all day if others question your teaching style or methods.

* You crave approval and well-deserved compliments for what you do. Getting recognition for your efforts is important to you.

* Minor incidents really bother you. You tend to report them to administration so they can deal with them.

* You meet everyone else's needs but at times quietly wonder if your own needs are being met.

* You work hard to ensure that parents, guardians, and grandparents are not only comfortable with you, but happy with you.

* You hate group projects with coworkers. You'd rather do them yourself, so they can be done perfectly…or not at all. You already have enough to deal with.

* You tend to compare how your students are doing with students in other classrooms in the same grade.

If this sounds the most like you, flip to pages 179-180 to see what you need most.

TEACHER #3

* You like routine, structure, and clear game plans.

* Meetings drive you crazy since they don't seem to accomplish much. Their agendas, if there are any, seem jumbled, last-minute, long-winded, and not respectful of your time.

* You have good results in the classroom because you do things the way you are used to doing them.

* Any training or workshop feels like a waste of your time. You've tried their tips, and they weren't successful. Ditto with tips from other teachers. They're tucked in your "Someday" file, but you don't feel led to put any of them into practice right away.

* You are comfortable with your tried-and-true teaching style and methods. Why change what is already working?

* You are content with being the head of your classroom and don't necessarily need or seek other relationships within the school.

* Other teachers and administrators have not often offered you help that was really *help*. You're used to that approach, and you don't expect or seek anything more.

* You feel fulfilled when your students are organized, respectful, and do the work you requested them to do.

If this sounds the most like you, flip to pages 181-182 to see what you need most.

TEACHER #4

* You were called to teach, and it's clearly your passion. You get tremendous joy knowing you can positively impact the next generation. You can't imagine doing anything else.

* You are confident in your teaching style, methods, and curriculum mastery.

* You have good results in the classroom.

* You see your students as individuals with varying skills and gifts, and consider it an honor to assist in fulfilling their unique potential.

* You have clear goals but vary how you accomplish them depending on your class makeup.

* You enjoy learning teaching methods and getting others' ideas and input. You desire to hone your craft, grow, develop, challenge yourself, and become the best teacher you can be.

* It's invigorating and fun to mentor new teachers and share secrets you've learned to make their early years more manageable. You might be interested in teaching a workshop on your school campus.

* You're known as an enthusiastic person who demonstrates school spirit and camaraderie.

* Your open-door policy allows students to chat with you, have lunch with you, or discuss a difficult homework assignment. You're often surrounded by students who need and hunger for a positive role model, empathy, and advice.

* Because you are skilled and so relational, sometimes you get asked to assist others too much.

If this sounds the most like you, flip to pages 183-184 to see what you need most.

A TEACHER'S MINDSET

One of the beauties of teaching
is that there is no limit
to one's growth as a teacher,
just as there is no knowing beforehand
how much your students can learn.
HERBERT KOHL

GOOD HABITS
MAKE GREAT TEACHERS.

We are what we repeatedly do.
Excellence, then, is not an act, but a habit.
ARISTOTLE

"What would the world be like without teachers?"

That was the question our school asked students recently. The results were shown in a video at the next teacher in-service day. Do you know what the top two answers by far were? "Chaos" and "sad."

I pondered those responses for a while before it hit me. What is the opposite of *chaos* and *sadness*? *Order* and *happiness*—the two ingredients I believe are most necessary for a successful classroom learning environment.

Why order? Order is crucial for classrooms. It helps foster a sense of safety, maintains discipline, and allows teachers to teach effectively. Order promotes student engagement, buy-in, pride in your school, and contributes to an overall positive campus atmosphere.

Establishing that order isn't always fun as first-year teachers will attest. It takes an awful lot of work, proactive planning, and experimenting to see what works for you. However, highlight order as a habit and soon it will become one, especially when you see the benefits in a smoothly running classroom.

Why is happiness so important? Happiness is what drives students to want to come to school, ready to delve into their class work. It prompts them to be kind to their peers. It pushes them to be a participant in their own learning. It encourages them to assist with community tasks to keep your classroom beautiful, clean, and organized. That includes tasks such as cleaning desks and boards, gathering trash, picking up after art projects, and placing papers in bins where they belong. It encourages them to dare to try something new instead of fearing being laughed at.

Other answers in the video that pulled at my heartstrings were "lonely" and "we'd have no one to learn with." On the days you aren't 100 percent pumped up to teach, you feel stuck in a rut, or you lose your motivation, remember those words. Your students need you. In fact, they're depending on you not only for order and happiness but for companionship and belonging.

The second question in the video was, "Who would you like to thank for encouraging you and believing in you?" The stories and words that followed were truly inspiring and at times prompted tears. Some students and teachers couldn't think of *anyone* to thank. They couldn't remember a single person who believed in them or encouraged them. Such a sobering reality is a good reminder to look for and engage with individuals who need an extra dose of encouragement and belief.

But here's the most important theme that came across to me in the video interviews. We as teachers are role models in everything. We are the ones who come early and stay late to provide order, organization, and a clear roadmap. We greet students with a smile as they enter and leave for the day. We treat grumpy students with respect and kindness. We exhibit a hard-work ethic. We are honest, admit our mistakes, and use those situations to enrich student perspectives and learning. We are steady when surprises occur and do our best to let our sense of humor reign.

Are all of these things easy to do? No, especially not on one of "those" days. The kind of distracted days that start out literally on the wrong foot when you look down and realize you are wearing two different colors of socks. Worse, you've forgotten your lunch. On those days, let's face it, you don't feel "excellent" or "social."

However, good habits practiced over and over make great teachers. A smooth-running classroom begins with a positive mindset, hours of brainstorming and organizing your materials, establishing routines and roadmaps with your students, and proactive methods of streamlining each day's chaos. It also comes from the realization that pursuing excellence is not the same as pursuing perfection. You can never attain perfection, unless you are God Almighty. But you can pursue excellence.

If you do these things, your classroom becomes a happy and safe space for students. A place with beneficial companionship on their journey of learning. A community where they can belong and make a positive contribution.

The process of teaching isn't a "one and done" activity. It is, as Aristotle said, "what we repeatedly do." At first that may seem discouraging. The job is never done. However, it's actually good news. You can have one bad day, laugh it off, and try again. You can attack the next day with determination to do and be better.

Developing good habits, tenacity, and a drive for excellence—yes, despite some failures—goes a long way toward instilling the same "can do" philosophy and good habits into your students. After all, your students are always watching their role model. What you do will speak more loudly than what you say. However, put together consistency in what you say and in what you do, and you set up good habits that will benefit you and your students for a lifetime.

Classroom Corner

* How might the idea "what we repeatedly do" encourage you to instill good habits in one particular area of teaching?
* Choose one of the four elements (order, happiness, sense of companionship, belonging) to work on in your classroom this week. At the end of the week, what changes do you see in yourself, your classroom, and your students as a result?

Teacher's Toolbelt

Change begins with you. Take a look around your room and especially your desk area. Does it reflect beauty and order?

Spend time after school straightening up your area and then require your students to do the same the next day. Model what order looks like by being organized yourself.

YOU ARE THE AUTHORITY AND CHANGE-MAKER IN THE CLASSROOM.

The mediocre teacher tells.
The good teacher explains.
The superior teacher demonstrates.
The great teacher inspires.
WILLIAM ARTHUR WARD

Teachers often ask me, "What do you do with a kid who goes out of his way to be sent to the principal's office? How can you curb that behavior?"

My response might surprise you. "Think about this for a second. Would *you* want to be a student in your classroom?"

You see, chances are if you've got a repeat offender, that student is creating some chaos on purpose to get out of class. Is your class really that boring? So boring that all he can think about is wandering down the school hallway toward the principal's office as a compelling and fun alternative?

Are your lectures so long that, as a kinesthetic-motion learner, he struggles to sit at his desk so creates a diversion? Is your classroom a rigid zone where any rule infraction exacts a heavy toll on the offender? Or a free-for-all zone where anything goes, rules are merely suggestions, and chaos reigns?

You can try all the "attitude adjustment" techniques in the world. However, if your class isn't an interesting, inspirational, and interactive place to be, students will want to be somewhere else.

But here's the good news. *You* are the authority in that classroom, and you have the power to change what you don't like. Take a good look at your classroom and teaching techniques. If you're so bored by your own material that you teach in autopilot, change it up. For your students to be engaged, you need to be engaged and enthusiastic about teaching the subject matter.

Do you have planned times where students can get up from their desks, stretch their legs, and interact with others while still learning? How about the temperature of your classroom? If you walked in the door and viewed your space with fresh eyes, does the environment feel warm and welcoming, yet structured?

Students need to see your authority and the classroom rules you set as good for all students, providing boundaries and safety. You can tell your students what to do all day long, but you gain nothing if those students don't have a prior good relationship with you. As we always say, "They don't care what you know, until they know that you care." Students who have a relationship with you want to stay in your classroom because they know it's the best place to be. Students whom others label "impossible" since they refuse to adhere to classroom rules can be amazingly transformed when you invest in them and win their cooperation.

How do you do that? It's simple. Show interest in your students as individuals and in what interests them. This only takes a minute or two a day but reaps exponential rewards in your relationship.

The next time a student acts up, don't send him trotting down the hall to the principal's office. Never abdicate your position of authority to anyone, whether parents, other teachers, students, or the principal. Unless safety is at stake, keep the student and any challenges in your court.

Instead call his bluff. Pull him aside privately. Say, "It seems you are working hard to get thrown out of class. Tell me more about why you feel you have to do that."

Most likely he'll get that caught-in-the-act look and be tongue-tied. You wait at least 30 seconds for any response. If there is none, you say softly, "Anytime you want to talk about that or anything that is bothering you, I'm here and ready to listen." Then you send him back to his seat with the kind of relational discipline that will have him still puzzling as he tries to get to sleep that night.

That, Teacher, is how you win friends and influence students for good.

Classroom Corner

* What was your favorite class when you were growing up? What did the teacher say or do that made it interesting? What kind of relationship did you have with that teacher?
* How might you incorporate similar strategies from that teacher into your classroom today?

Teacher's Toolbelt

Maybe you are thinking, *They don't get the kids I have in my class.* Or, *They don't know what type of kids and behaviors we get every day in my class.*

You are right. We haven't been to your class. But we likely have visited one that is very similar. What is the same, regardless of the students you serve, is the basic need for all of us to be loved and accepted.

Relationships with those around us matter. As you reflect on your own education and a teacher who impacted you, consider how that teacher made you feel. Are you emulating that same feeling in your class with your students?

Let's face it. If you give off the persona that you don't care and would rather be elsewhere, it's going to be an uphill battle. But if you are encouraging, sincere, and accepting, your students will start to notice that there is something different about you.

Be consistent. Don't take any guff from your students. But base all you do on positive relationships. Attend a ball game when your student is playing, go to their dance recital, or invest in a new paintbrush for that budding artist.

The point is to show interest in what they are interested in. They will come around. Relationships take time and trust.

PRINCIPLE #3

KNOW YOURSELF, KNOW YOUR CLASS.

Knowing others is intelligence;
knowing yourself is true wisdom.
LAO TZU

Did you know that the student you're most likely to like and also clash with is the one who's most like you? And that clash has everything to do with birth order? Understanding your own birth order and how birth orders mix and match also helps you relate uniquely to each student so you can form a relationship that outlasts challenges during the year.

What's your birth order? It's the order in which you were born or adopted into the family you grew up in. Here's a quick primer of some birth order characteristics. (For those inquiring minds wanting to know more, see *The Birth Order Book* by Dr. Kevin Leman.)

Firstborn: Lucky you, to have all your parents' attention for a while. But as their guinea pig, everything you did, right or wrong, was heightened. You became an achiever, leader, and perfectionist, hard on others but hardest on yourself. You're logical, well organized, have a strong sense of justice, and take life seriously. You hate surprises.

Only born: You're everything a firstborn is but with extra doses of self-motivation, stress, and high achievement. You think in black and white, use words like *always* and *never*, and constantly raise the high bar on yourself. You don't tolerate nonsense of any kind.

Middleborn: Squished between firstborn star and entertaining baby, you mediated between those warring parties enough that you learned to retreat if a fight brewed. Wanting life's roads to be smooth, you avoid conflicts and compromise rather than provoking a fight. You're often elusive in your "we'll see..." answers instead of stating yes or no.

Lastborn: Engaging and affectionate, you love people, activities, surprises, and the limelight but sometimes dodge responsibility. You were a pro at getting siblings or a parent to do your work by acting helpless or disappearing to play. Since you were "cute," siblings often got blamed for what you did because they were older, should know better, and let you get in trouble.

Just as these characteristics are likely true of you (see *The Birth Order Book* for specifics and reasons for variations), they're also true of your students. That's where the clashing occurs. You will always over-identify with the students in the same birth order as you, putting too much pressure on them or favoring them too much.

How does this play out in the classroom? Let's say two students start slinging words. How will you respond differently based on your birth order and the students' birth orders?

Firstborns will tend to make snap decisions about who's at fault. Your eagle eye will hold the firstborn student responsible because she ought to know better (even though you hated it when your parents did that to you). Since two firstborns like issues defined and settled and have a strong sense of justice, you two will understandably butt heads. Your critical eye also might zoom in on the lastborn since your little sister tended to get away with everything.

Onlies spout an infamous line: "Can't you all just get along?" Competition and fighting among students is frankly as inevitable as death and taxes. Sometimes you have to let go of those classroom ideals and let your students tussle it out within the boundaries of respect and structure required as part of your class community.

Middleborns hate disharmony, so you step in to smooth things over. "Now, kids, what is this all about?" Such attempts fuel any complaint fest. You also will tend to jump to any middleborn's defense, since you know what it's like to be stuck in the middle of a fight. But remember this: fighting is an act of *cooperation* since it takes two or more to tango.

Lastborns swoop in like avenging angels to defend the youngest, most helpless-acting student. Yes, you got away with a lot yourself, but you have vivid memories of siblings pounding on you when Mom or Dad wasn't looking. However, accept the reality that the lastborn likely did *something* to fuel that tussle.

How do you handle such a situation? You rein in gut instincts as judge and jury. Instead, you put the warring students in the driver's seat of that event. When two fighters have to face each other eye-to-eye and problem-solve together, it's amazing how swiftly the truth comes out and conflicts fizzle.

Classroom Corner

* What pros of your birth order serve you well in the classroom and how? Consider:

> Firstborn tendencies of organization and leadership?
>
> Only-born tendencies of self-motivation and project completion?
>
> Middleborn tendencies of diplomatic mediation?
>
> Lastborn tendencies of charisma and fun as a priority?

* How might knowing your birth order help you to think beyond the moment? Such as not liking surprises as a firstborn, being a

perfectionist as an only born, being independent as a middleborn, or craving limelight and approval as a lastborn?

Teacher's Toolbelt

Did you know that birth order should impact the way you do your seating charts? That's especially true for middle and high-school students.

Assign two firstborns to work together on a project, and they'll be like prize fighters in a ring, competing for the "Most Detailed" title and sparring for a knockout blow. Assign two middleborns, and they'll tip-toe around their ideas, afraid to offend the other. Assign two lastborns, and they'll bond socially, tell stories, and laugh instead of working.

But seat a firstborn and lastborn together, and the firstborn will gain confidence in directing a project while the lastborn will learn that he can and should contribute. Seat a firstborn and a middleborn together, and the firstborn will learn that others also have ideas worth considering while the middleborn will learn how to stand up for his ideas. Seat a middleborn and a lastborn together, and the middleborn's mediator skills will provide that lastborn desired attention and social interaction while the lastborn introduces ripples of fun in the smooth waters of the middleborn.

Why not try some combinations and see for yourself?

If you think the concept of birth order is overrated, then do this: seat four lastborns together in the back of your classroom. Make sure to provide the peanuts and popcorn for the rest of the class because there will be a constant circus going on free of charge. Now isn't that useful information to keep chaos down to a minimum in your classroom?

CULTIVATE AN ORGANIZED MIND AND SYSTEM.

Everything is easier when you're organized.
You can get to work faster without wasting time looking for stuff.
NEMOURS CHILDREN'S HEALTH

Have you ever been in front of your class and realized that you neglected to get the math manipulatives out of the back closet that you needed for the lesson? You tell the class to chat with each other about what they did this past weekend while you begin to find the needed manipulatives. What happens next? The volume in your classroom goes up because you have lost your students' attention. You've also wasted class time trying to locate your items, and now you feel frazzled.

The reality is, organization and preplanning greatly impacts the quality of your instruction and the overall education of your students. What do you do when such an event occurs? You can use it as a teachable moment.

Here's how that works. You pause and tell the class you take responsibility for not being prepared. You might share how you felt as you realized your mistake. Let them see that you are human. Of course, such disorganization can't happen every day or you'll lose credibility. But when it does happen on occasion, be real. Be honest. Then get back to work as fast as possible.

Organization is a critical skill for teachers. That includes organizing your materials, your classroom space, and your time. Master those three areas of organization, and you'll be amazed at how good you feel at the start of every school day.

Today is the day to start making baby steps toward your end goal. One game changer is implementing a system that allows you to have everything you need for the day or week in one place. Every teacher organizes differently. The good news is that there are multiple tools to choose from. Maybe you prefer hanging files, baskets, binders, cubbies, or any other organizational system. As long as that system works for you, that's all that matters.

When I was first teaching in the classroom, I made it a point to never leave for the day until I was prepared for the following day. As my experience in the classroom increased, that changed to never leaving on a Friday afternoon until I was 100 percent planned and prepared for the entire following week. I could then enjoy my weekend and still be confident that I had everything ready for stepping back into the classroom on Monday morning.

Why not try out those techniques for yourself? They're both great ways to wrap up the day or the week with a big smile. And they'll ensure that you begin the next day or week with confidence and a bigger smile. You'll be ready the minute your students walk through that classroom door. What's not to like about that?

Classroom Corner

* Take a look at your teacher table right now. Is it clean and organized with supplies ready for student learning? Or are there stacks of papers to be graded and items you need to put away? Is your table more of a storage space than a teaching environment?

If so, it's time to try out some organizational tips we've shared. If yours is perfectly clean and organized, pat yourself on the back. Keep these ideas in your back pocket for one of "those days" that we all have.

* Which of the three areas (stuff, space, or time) is most difficult for you to organize? What goal can you set for yourself this week?

At the end of the week, do a quick evaluation of how you did that week. Celebrate what worked and change what didn't.

Teaching isn't about perfection. It's about pursuing excellence.

Teacher's Toolbelt

Time can be a major factor in a school setting. The number-one complaint of teachers usually is, "There just isn't enough time." So why not use the time you have at school to your advantage?

Recruit parent volunteers and use your planning time efficiently during the school day. I know how tempting it is to pop into the class next door and chat with your fellow teacher. After all, a break from work is nice. But the reality is, if you don't get your work done now, you'll have more to do later. And that later includes school nights and weekends when you need and deserve some personal time.

Consider how much homework you are assigning and the length of time it will take to grade each of those assignments. Perhaps be more creative in your formative and summative assessments so you can get a better idea of how your students are progressing without having to grade quizzes and tests every night.

If you need help with organization, there's usually an expert not far down the hall who has it all figured out. It's the room you pass as you walk your kids to gym and sigh every time you see it. You wonder, *How does she do it?*

Well, why not ask if you can peruse her room for organizational ideas? Or ask if she'd mind stepping into your room to give you some tips for organizing a specific area of your space? The majority of teachers would be happy to share their ideas and tips.

As a bonus, you might share a chuckle or two at ideas you've tried that didn't work. There's nothing like a little laughter over missteps to lighten both of your days.

KEEP SUGGESTIONS AND CRITICISM IN PERSPECTIVE.

Appreciate the constructive;
ignore the destructive.
JOHN DOUGLAS

A newbie teacher once asked me, "How often should I take other teachers' suggestions? When should I stick with my gut of what I should do?" Barraged with criticism from others in the field about her methods, she doubted her own skills and ideas.

Teachers who have been in the field for a few or many years tend to be helpful by nature. They've been in your shoes and have learned a lot along their educational journeys. They've fallen down, picked themselves back up, and don't want others to stumble unnecessarily. They've also tried—sometimes successfully, sometimes not so successfully—a variety of strategies and have their tricks-of-the-trade to share with you.

At times in their zest to come to your aid, those teachers might forget that you crave the same autonomy they have over their own classrooms. They might also forget Malcolm Gladwell's wise words: "Criticism is a privilege that you earn—it shouldn't be your opening move in an interaction." In other words, the words you choose to say and how they are interpreted by the other party have everything to do with the relationship you've already established.

Any suggestion or criticism needs to be *constructive,* not *destructive.* How can you know the difference? Ask yourself a simple question: *How do I feel after this encounter?* Do you feel included as part of the group, affirmed, and energized to tackle that issue, project, or area with some fresh perspective and ideas? If so, the feedback was constructive. Do you want to hide somewhere to regroup from the onslaught of words? If so, the feedback was destructive.

Constructive criticism focuses on *assisting* you. It offers guidance in an *objective* manner, focusing on the issue at hand. The words are respectful, uplifting, sensitive, and empathetic to your situation. Constructive criticism uplifts you while offering possible solutions, should a similar situation come up in the future. It has a "hey, no one's perfect, and we're all in this together" kind of tone.

Destructive criticism focuses on *degrading* you. It directs negative language toward you in a *subjective* manner, focusing on you as the mistake or failure instead of the issue at hand. Destructive criticism is condescending, condemning, and does not help you problem-solve. It has a "you're such a failure that there's no hope for you" kind of tone.

When facing destructive criticism, keep in mind Marshall Rosenberg's assessment: "Analyses of others are actually expressions of our own needs and values." So if, for example, another teacher launches a blast of criticism at you for allowing your class to be noisy in the hallway, she is likely a firstborn or only-born individual with a high sense of order and a penchant for control. She cannot stand anyone coloring outside the lines or tampering with her rulebook. Understanding such a basic fact will assist you in keeping such criticism in perspective.

It's always good to be open to suggestions and constructive criticism. However, being open is not the same thing as being controlled by others' words and subsequently doubting your own skills and ideas.

What should you do the next time a well-intentioned (or a not-so-well-intentioned) fellow teacher gives you feedback? Smile. Thank that person for their suggestions. Say you'll think about those ideas. Never respond to criticism, whether constructive or destructive, with criticism.

As you walk away from that encounter, ponder their suggestions. Ask yourself, *Are those suggestions valid? Would they help? Have I tried that strategy before? How did it work or not work?* If you haven't tried it and think it might work, why not give it a try?

If that teacher later oversteps her bounds and follows up to ask how the suggestion worked, smile again. Say you appreciated the suggestion and have lots of methods to try. Then politely say you think you now have a good handle on your class and a variety of strategies to employ. Thank her for their willingness to walk alongside you. Then exit stage-left, walking confidently at a comfortable pace with a happy heart.

Politeness and charm go a long way in winning friends and neighbors.

Classroom Corner

* In what area(s) of teaching do you feel less confident and tend to second-guess yourself? Why? How important is others' approval to you? Joyce Meyer once quipped, "The best way to get along with people is not to expect them to like you." How might you use constructive criticism from others as a tool for growth?

* Reflect on Rosenberg's statement, "Analyses of others are actually expressions of our own needs and values." How might that assessment assist you in thinking how best to approach other teachers with your assessments, suggestions, or critiques?

Teacher's Toolbelt

Let's face it. Teaching is personal. You invest your time, energy, and resources. You devote much of your life to this great profession. It can be hard to receive feedback that is less than complimentary to that all-encompassing work.

Embrace the fact that you need grit in order to grow. "No grit, no pearl," as an unknown author once said. I believe that with all my heart. In fact, I often use that quote to correspond with the teachers I now serve.

You know yourself best. Reflect on any feedback, whether solicited or not, to grow in your profession and positively impact students. Have that perspective, and your potential to grow is exponential.

PRINCIPLE #6

ASKING FOR HELP IS A SIGN OF SMARTNESS.

Don't be afraid to ask for help when you need it....
Asking for help isn't a sign of weakness, it's a sign of strength.
It shows you have the courage to admit when you don't know something,
and to learn something.
BARACK OBAMA

Every single day teachers are miracle workers who are often expected to be the jack of all trades. That's especially true if you're a K-5 teacher. Unlike many of your middle-school and high-school counterparts, you are responsible for teaching multiple subjects.

Let's be honest, shall we? Each of us has particular gifts that assist us in excelling in specific areas. Each of us also lacks gifts in other areas. For example, those who excel in making history and language classes fascinating and lively may struggle in the areas of science and math.

Asking for help when you need it is a sign of smartness, not weakness. It showcases that you are a lifelong learner and want to continue to improve your skills. For that, we applaud you. Such tenacity and determination will power you on in the field of education.

But how can you get the targeted help you need?

First, *risk asking*. Individuals often don't ask for help because they assume the other person might say no. No one likes to be rejected. But here's what you need to know. In general, people like to be useful to others, appreciate being asked, and are typically willing to help.

Second, *clarify the type of help you'd like before you ask for help.* Pre-write a simple list of what you need so you can be specific in your ask. Such an action will focus your thoughts and allow you to communicate succinctly to make the best use of your time with that person.

Third, *think carefully who to ask.* Granted, you might need to talk to multiple people. However, who might be the best one to start with to gain information you could benefit from? Such upfront consideration will keep you from getting overwhelmed with ideas that haven't yet been tested in the fires of the classroom.

If you aren't comfortable talking to your own team first, search out a person in your building who is masterful in the area you need assistance with. Ask if she or he would be willing to let you come watch a lesson or perhaps have a brief chat about it after school. You can stretch your wings more by asking a coworker or administrator to come watch your lesson and provide you with constructive feedback.

Fourth, *ask that person in a way he or she cannot say no.* The simple statement, "I'm wondering if you would help me with something…" is a great way to begin. It's polite and respectful. It gets that person's attention and your request is easy for them to understand.

When you get that "Sure, what do you need?" response (which you likely will, unless that teacher has had a very bad day), use your simple list. Be clear and concise. Explain why you need help. Be specific about what you need and that you believe this person could assist you. Clarify what you hope to achieve.

Make sure your "ask" is doable for a person with a busy schedule. Consider the following asks on the same issue:

> *Ask 1:* "I am looking for someone to mentor me on teaching reluctant readers."

Ask 2: "I'm wondering if you could give me 20 minutes after school someday in the next couple of weeks to share a few tips for motivating the reluctant readers in my class."

If someone approached you with the first ask, you'd likely head for the hills as nicely and swiftly as possible. Why? Because the ask is broad-based and nebulous in its time commitment. Looking for "someone" (translate that as "anyone") shows desperation instead of carefully targeted consideration of which person might best be able to help.

If someone approached you with the second ask, you'd likely say, "No problem. I'd love to help. How about next Tuesday?" Why the swift response? Because the ask is specific, targeted, and doable.

Who knows? Such an exchange might be the beginning of a strong relationship and healthy flow of ideas that not only feels good but assists both of you in excelling in your craft.

Classroom Corner

* In what area(s) of teaching would you benefit from doing the ask? What specifically do you need assistance with?
* What's your plan for targeting your need, the person to ask, and making the exchange doable?

Teacher's Toolbelt

Imagine this situation…

Your school assigns you an "Instructional Coach." You've never been a fan of people watching you teach and you feel anxious. You wonder, *Am I in trouble? Are they truly coming to help? Or are they evaluating me to decide if I'm in or out for next year?*

It's normal to feel anxious and question the motivation behind such a move. However, working alongside an Instructional Coach doesn't mean you're in trouble. In fact, if your school has assigned one to you, they aren't looking to oust you. They think you're worth investing in and are proactively providing more tools for your growing teacher toolbelt.

That coach is there to help you improve your craft, reflect on your teaching practices, encourage you to try new strategies, and improve student outcomes. So why not take advantage of this opportunity? Embrace it. Trust the process. Think of it as having your own individual expert assigned a box seat in your classroom to observe all the goings-on and give you tips, all at no cost to you.

Good instructional coaches walk alongside you as encouragers. They ask meaningful questions that reflect your decisions and values as a teacher. You can assist by jotting down questions you want to discuss with your coach and keeping a notebook of your conversations. Do that and in a short time you'll be amazed how much your teaching has improved. And you'll feel awfully good about the results too.

SET YOUR GOALS
AND STICK TO THEM.

*Set your goal, don't give up when you face obstacles,
and stay focused, as the power within is truly amazing!*
CATHERINE PULSIFER

If there were one goal you could accomplish this year, what would it be? Identifying that goal is the first step. Then to meet that goal you need both strategy and tactics.

Strategy defines your long-term goals in the classroom and how you're planning to achieve them. It provides the path and vision required to achieve your mission as an educator.

Tactics are short-term actions you take to achieve that long-term vision. They're much more concrete than strategy. Tactics are specific steps and detailed plans that need to be accomplished in order to complete the overall strategy.

The best way to explain the difference between the two is that you must think strategically but act tactically in approaching any goal.

Goals can come in all shapes and sizes and vary throughout the course of the school year. For example, maybe in the first days of a new school year, you set a goal to learn all your students' names and one unique fact about each of them. This is the beginning of relationship building.

As you look to academics, you set goals that are attainable and will have a high impact on your classroom culture and student outcomes. Maybe you want to introduce one new small group activity or read more about a topic that would impact your instruction. Goals that are too vague and too large are not attainable and can make you feel defeated. One foot in front of the other to the goal is a safe and sturdy path to achievement.

Most of all, whatever goal you set must be important to *you*. If someone else prescribes your goal, you'll lack the needed buy-in to make it happen. Be realistic in setting your goals. It's sometimes the little things we do that help us accomplish big tasks.

When I set goals for myself for the upcoming school year, I would break down my broader goals into smaller, more manageable pieces. I looked at certain distinctives as they related to curriculum and instruction and then began formulating goals that would have high impact on teachers and students. After reviewing and tweaking those goals, I landed at a place where I was comfortable. I knew that the goals would stretch me but were attainable.

Next, I created a document that listed each goal and the needed action steps. I placed the sheet in an acrylic frame that sits by my desk. I reference that sheet often to keep me focused and on track. I also check off the goals with an Expo marker as I complete them. Doing that gives meaning and purpose to my work. Every time I get to check a goal off, I feel a sense of accomplishment.

Have a goal you'd like to meet? Mark Twain said it well: "The secret of getting ahead is getting started." To meet a goal, you first have to set it and then stick to it. Do that, and you'll be amazed at what you accomplish.

Let's say you set a goal after listening to a podcast that discussed increased wait time and the impact it has on students' engagement. You want to test that theory, so you set a goal to increase your wait time to five seconds after asking a question. You ask your questions and then count slowly in your head to five before calling on a student to answer.

If you want to take that goal a step further, invite a colleague into your classroom. Have him watch a lesson and note your wait time. Ask for feedback and discuss the impact that implementing an increased wait time had on your classroom and on your students.

If you are not comfortable inviting a colleague or administrator into your classroom, why not record one of your lessons yourself? Set your phone up in an inconspicuous place in the room. Review the recording later to evaluate your use of wait time.

Yes, we know. Watching yourself can be a little uncomfortable. But that slight pain will be worth it. Such an exercise will open your eyes to things happening in the classroom that you might miss otherwise.

Now it's your turn. What goal would you like to accomplish in the classroom? How might you be able to think strategically? What steps and plans could you make to act tactically?

You won't know what you can do until you get started. We can't wait to see you fly off that runway.

Classroom Corner

* Steve Jobs once said, "If you are working on something that you really care about, you don't have to be pushed. The vision pulls you." What vision is pulling you?

* How might you pursue that vision with strategy? What tactics would help you implement that vision?

Teacher's Toolbelt

Think of your own learning style and consider what might be helpful for you to achieve your goals. If you are an auditory learner, record your goals to yourself in a friendly, encouraging message you can listen to once a week. Check your progress for the week against those goals.

If you are a visual learner, make sure you write those goals down. List any action steps you will take for each one. Keep that list in a place where you can reference it easily and quickly.

Above all, set an end date so you have a focus to your work. Ask a trusted colleague to check in with you regarding your goal.

COUNT TO 10 BEFORE YOU RESPOND TO AN ANGRY PARENT.

Speak when you are angry,
and you will make the best speech you'll ever regret.
LAURENCE J. PETER

Parents of your students can sometimes be all too human. They will react instead of respond to a situation. A teacher we'll call "Kenzie" once received a very angry email from a parent who wasn't happy with a recent assignment she had given. The mother felt it was too difficult, too long, and too much to ask for a child her daughter's age.

Kenzie was stunned at the accusatory tone of the email. She'd thought she had developed a good relationship with that parent since the beginning of the year. To make things worse, the parent was pretty influential at her school. "What should I do?" Kenzie asked me.

"We've all been there," I told her. "In fact, I found myself in a similar situation early on in my teaching career. Not only was I upset by the email and hurt by its tone and message, I questioned how that particular assignment could cause such an uproar. I had a hunch that something was off, and I chose to follow that hunch."

Then I told her the rest of the story. The first break I had in my classroom, I phoned that parent. I calmly told her that I had received her message and wanted to better understand what caused such frustration for her and her child. What happened next totally shocked me.

The parent apologized for zipping off that email and claimed total responsibility for it. She told me they had forgotten about the due date until the previous night. Because she was so frazzled, she had paid her older child to complete the assignment for her younger daughter. Whoa. I didn't expect that revelation, but once I heard the real issue, the vitriol in the email made sense.

But think what might have happened if I had reacted instead of responded. What's the difference? When you react, you let your emotions and mouth fly before your logic and the consideration of consequences kicks in. In Kenzie's and my situations with parents, reacting could have prompted a flurry of tit-for-tat escalation of emotion-laden emails rather than getting to the heart of the issue. It could have derailed our developing relationships with the parents and made addressing any issue regarding their children more difficult throughout the remainder of the year.

When you respond, you choose to control any gut reactions. You allow your emotions to calm by counting to 10. You reread an email. You allow time to evaluate the situation. You think, *Are the words I'm hearing or seeing via text or email the whole story? What am I missing here?*

My advice to you, and any other teachers who find themselves in yours and my shoes, is never to engage in a text or an email exchange with a person who is upset. Instead, take a few steadying breaths. Eat some dark chocolate since it's known to boost happy, calm feelings.[1] Think through what you are going to say to introduce the topic, keeping in mind the importance of a year-long relationship with that parent. Then pick up the phone and call.

I know calling is hard to do in such situations. But, trust me, the outcome of this action with a let's-solve-this-together tone is usually very positive. Often you learn something about your student and her home life that can assist you in the future. You are also able to ratchet down the temperature of the situation and resolve it swiftly before any frustrations pass from that parent to any other parent.

Such a problem-solving team approach is a win-win. You understand more about the potential pitfalls of an assignment and can assess any concerns to see if that assignment or its deadline needs to be adjusted. Hopefully the parent learns a lesson or two about not speaking her mind and hitting a send button before she lets a few minutes go by and rereads that email or text.

Above all, let grace reign. That parent will likely be embarrassed the next time you see her. Smile and greet her kindly, and she'll be more than relieved. That little step of letting bygones be bygones will go a long way in building your relationship with her…and clearing the path for any other issues that might crop up later in the school year.

Classroom Corner

* The next time you face a reactive parent, how might you respond instead? Try role-playing a potential scenario with a friend, fellow teacher, or family member.

* A bagel-shop owner once posted this sign for her employees: "It takes a long time to win a customer's loyalty, and only one negative interaction to lose that relationship." How might this perspective assist you in staying calm and pursuing a problem-solving approach with parents or guardians?

Teacher's Toolbelt

When you're caught off guard and don't know how to respond, it can be wise to say something like, "You raise a good point. Let me look into that and get back to you." Give yourself time to process and investigate other perspectives. Dig in deeper to ensure you have the information needed to inform your decision. That doesn't mean you have to change your mind or back down on an issue.

Above all, make sure you do respond. Otherwise, you'll lose credibility. When you respond promptly, offer new information, and proceed in a manner that is beneficial and not harmful to your relationship, you'll soar in the eyes of that parent.

"Let me get back to you." Those words are simple to remember. Most of all, they lessen the potential for letting words fly that you might later wish you could recall.

BE INTENTIONAL AND POSITIVELY TRANSFORMATIONAL.

No one cares how much you know
until they know how much you care.
THEODORE ROOSEVELT

I have a bad habit: McDonald's Diet Coke. In fact, I pass a McDonald's on my drive to school and find myself in the drive-thru most mornings.

It's not only the fresh cup of Diet Coke I'm seeking, though. It's the sunshiny spirit of Elizabeth, the drive-thru attendant whom I hope to interact with each day. Over my daily visits I've gotten to know her. I pull up to the drive-thru, hear her cheery voice, greet her by name, and suddenly even a cloudy day is brighter.

You see, Elizabeth knows my voice, my name, and my order. But, most importantly, she knows how to make a person feel good.

Each day she replies to me with intentional positivity. "Good morning, Sunshine! Large Diet Coke?" Or sometimes she says, "Good morning, Krissy!" or "Good morning, Beautiful!"

I reply with the same order of "Large Diet Coke" each day. Then I proceed to the checkout window. We share a positive exchange for the day and an "I'll see you tomorrow." It's a brief blip in time, but I always leave that window feeling energized.

After a recent visit, I drove away contemplating the cost of positivity. It costs Elizabeth nothing to be positive with me. Ditto with what it costs me to be positive with Elizabeth. What if I never asked her name? What if I never chatted with her each day as she went about doing her job on my order? What if I didn't give her a smile and encouragement back?

If my interactions were her were merely *transactional* and not *transformational,* we'd both lose out on an opportunity to encourage and be encouraged with positivity to start our days. What's the difference?

If you are merely *transactional,* you expect that if you give something, you will receive something back. Nothing more, nothing less. In other words, you pay for your Diet Coke and you get that Diet Coke. You drive away from the window with the minimum of personal interaction. You go about your day unchanged except for the boost of energy your Diet Coke brings.

But if you are *transformational,* you are able to connect with others and evoke a positive change in them. That change can also influence other areas of that person's life. My exchange with Elizabeth propels me into my day sunny-side-up, ready to tackle any challenge. I hope I do the same for her.

Transformation also occurs in the classroom when a teacher is intentional and positively *transformational* in her interactions. How does that work?

Sarah, one of your students, enters your classroom. You can sense that something is not right. You quickly find yourself at the Y in the road. You have to choose between the transactional path and the transformational path in approaching her.

If you veer to the side of the transactional, you might say, "Sarah, I need you to get your math book out. We are getting started here, and you don't seem to be keeping up with us today."

Imagine what transpires next. Do you think Sarah's behavior and attitude will get better…or worse?

Now let's try the other path: the transformational one. As your other students are getting settled at their task, you walk casually up to Sarah's desk. You bend down and do a quick and quiet check-in with her. You mention that you've noticed something seems to be bothering her.

"I'd love to chat with you after class or during lunch, if you'd like to talk," you say empathetically. Then you add, "For now, do your best to get started on math."

Such words send a strong but kind message. You see her. You understand something is wrong. You are available to chat if she would like to, but you're not being pushy. Then you add the reality: even when we're not feeling our best, there's still work to be done.

Choosing to be intentionally positive is a powerful tool. As positivity leader Jon Gordon says, "Being positive doesn't just make you better; it makes everyone around you better."[2]

Classroom Corner

* Are you viewed as a positive person others like to be around? If so, smile as you think of an example or two. Then keep on doing what you are doing. If not, what would it cost you to be positive? Why not try it out today?

* How might the intentional power of positivity influence you personally? What impact might it have on your students, your classroom environment, your interactions with fellow teachers and administration, and the campus as a whole?

Teacher's Toolbelt

Plan a mini-workshop-getaway to investigate Jon Gordon's "7 Steps" to a Positive You.

1. Pull out your Telescope: Create your Vision.

2. Know your Why? What is your purpose?

3. Pull out your Microscope: What one action will you take?

4. Feed the Positive Dog: Stay Positive!

5. Neutralize the Energy Vampires.

6. Choose One Word.

7. #LoveServeCare.[3]

Think through each of the 7 Steps (for more on these and many other tools from positivity leader Jon Gordon, see endnote) and write down your ideas and plans.

Afterwards, post your "One Word" and the word *Positive* where you can see it every day. For further empowerment, review your notes on a monthly basis.

IT'S ALL ABOUT RELATIONSHIPS.

My teacher gave me the best gifts of all…
being consistent in what she said and did,
and, most of all, believing in me.
UNKNOWN

It's true. Teachers really can change the world. A teacher who understands relationships not only influences a child's buy-in to her education but captures her heart and wins her cooperation. And then, oh, the things that child will want to pursue wholeheartedly in that classroom once she knows that someone in her life believes in her.

You see, motivating a student is all about relationships: how she feels about herself, how she feels about others, and especially how she feels about you. That's why it's important to keep four things in mind each day you step into the classroom.

#1: Realize you are always a role model. Do you say what you mean and mean what you say? Are you consistent in your words and actions? Eyes are watching, and ears are listening. You are far more significant to your students than you may think.

What character qualities are you role-modeling today in speech and action? Kindness? Respect? Patience? Honesty? An I'll-never-give-up-despite-the-odds spirit?

#2: Minimize friction, optimize solutions. It's easy to react. Just open your mouth and spew without thinking. It's a lot harder to choose

how to respond. You have to stop to think about what you're saying, how you're saying it, and how your words might impact your listener.

Always remember that it takes two to tango. You don't have to play your student's (or their parent's) game. You be the adult.

Sometimes saying nothing is the best thing. If steam is about to blow, simply take a deep breath and smile. It'll buy you time to think if the interaction is in person. If it's via text or email, don't respond until you have considered potential responses and their relational consequences. Some words are better not said, and some actions are better left undone.

Here are two tricks of the trade that you can easily employ. Saying "you could be right" is an amazing argument deflator. Using what I call "escape clauses" will prevent you from saying the wrong thing prematurely and give you time to think. Try, "That's an interesting idea. Let me think on that. I'll get back to you."

Overall, the best way to minimize friction is to be kind and straightforward. Become an excellent communicator. Say what you mean, mean what you say, and then follow through on what you say you will do. Never forget that the words you choose to use and the tone in which you say them is extremely important to win the other party's cooperation.

Kids aren't dumb. They will gather from that tone how you feel about them. Which will it be? *My teacher must think I'm the dumbest person on the planet and not worth anything.* Or, *my teacher really likes me and has my back.*

#3: Plan well but roll with surprises. There will always be curveballs. Some will be doozies. You've likely experienced a few already. No amount of planning could have prepared you for those situations. Some important tools in a teacher's toolbelt are flexibility, adaptability,

and perspective. When surprises happen and you handle them well, good things can result, including valuable life lessons.

The next time you get thrown a curveball, remember what basketball coach John Wooden said: "Things work out best for those who make the best of how things work out." Do that, and you'll be the classroom that all the other teachers talk about with envy in the teachers' break room. "Wow, did you hear what happened in (name's) classroom? But, you know, he pulled the solution out of his hat like a magician. I wish I were that quick thinking and fast on my feet…."

#4: Stay the course. Teachers who don't give up when the going is tough can help students accomplish what seems impossible. How do you stay the course? Believe every day, in spite of evidence to the contrary, that you can be an instrument of change in the lives of your students.

Pursuing change, or in some cases transformation, isn't easy. Your students and their parents won't always like you during that process, especially if you do what's in their best interests. We all like to be liked. But approval is more important to some of us than others.

If you care deeply what others think of you, you'll need to work harder to keep others' words and attitudes from impacting your words and attitudes. Here's some great advice from author-speaker Joyce Meyer: "The best way to get along with people is not to expect them to like you." If you don't expect people to like you, then you'll be pleasantly surprised when and if they do. Now that's a freeing concept.

Each of the four things we've just shared has a similar element. That element is *Relationship.* Everything in your classroom is about relationships. Relationships first. Relationships always. No transformation can take place without relationships.

Classroom Corner

* Which one of the four things is the biggest challenge for you? How might you expand your proficiency in that area?

* Which student most needs your belief right now? What could you say and do to show that student that you expect and believe the best of him?

Teacher's Toolbelt

The time you invest in students is never wasted. In fact, being sincere and authentic in your relationships could save you countless hours in the long run. A great way to engage is through a "Lunch Bunch."

Choose a small group of students to have a picnic lunch with you. During that time, don't ask any questions about school. Instead, get to know those students as individuals. Listen to what they are interested in.

Continue your weekly "Lunch Bunch" until you've met with all your students. This type of relationship building allows each student to feel special and noticed. Understand each individual as a person first, and you'll be more equipped to meet his or her unique educational needs.

CLASSROOM STRATEGIES

*I entered the classroom with the conviction
that it was crucial for me and every other student
to be an active participant, not a passive consumer...
education that connects the will to know
with the will to become.*
BELL HOOKS

START OFF
ON THE RIGHT FOOT.

The will to succeed is important,
but what's more important is the will to prepare.
BOBBY KNIGHT

I look forward to "Back to School Night" every year. It's a great opportunity to meet my students' parents and guardians and welcome them not only to a new school year but to my classroom. It's also the best time to set the roadmap for the year, so I prepare carefully.

My opening question is this: "Over the last 180 days, have you ever had to correct your child for anything?" The answers inevitably come in the form of laughter, head-shakings, eye-rolls, and exchanges of empathetic looks.

That question might at first sound absurd. But it accomplishes a very important goal. It gets teacher and parents on an even playing field because, of course, the honest answer is a resounding "yes." No child is perfect. Neither is a parent or teacher.

Such a question serves as a good reminder that a child might from time to time need to be redirected, especially in a setting where they are part of a larger community. Parents need to know how you will inform them of concerns, how you will handle any discipline, and that any correction will always be done with respect and the child's long-term best interests in mind. If the issue isn't swiftly resolved or the behavior impacts the safety of the individual or others, the parent or guardian will be the first to know.

Parents also need to know your philosophy on education, including that grades and tests scores don't tell the whole story, and that failure and missteps can pave the path to success. They need to know your view of students as individuals who will be held responsible and accountable for their own learning and their contribution to the class as a whole. There's nothing like stating your expectations for the class upfront to bring a reality check to parents who think their darling is perfect and can do no wrong.

Every school year requires transitions for teacher, students, and parents. These include getting to know routines and schedules, tackling a higher level of learning from the previous year, and learning how to engage with a new mix of students who have differing personalities and life experiences.

If you teach young children, set parental expectations that the transition to part-time or full-time school can be challenging. Assure parents that the first week may be difficult, but this too shall pass. Kindergarten teachers always have at least one student who has a hard time. It can be more difficult if the child is a firstborn or only born leaving the safety of the nest and glimpsing a roomful of peers that he or she is not used to navigating.

Scenes often include lots of tears, a refusal to enter your classroom, or running and hiding to delay the inevitable. There's nothing more difficult for a kindergarten teacher than lining up the class on the first day of school and having one or more students start to cry. Why?

When I was teaching kindergarten, I learned that a single crying student had the potential to start a chain reaction. Soon other students began crying. Still, school had to start, and life had to go on. Children had to be dislodged from their parent's pant-legs.

What can you do in such cases? Reassure the family that the student will be okay. Tell them that crying and wanting to go home sometimes happens at this age during transition. Promise to call them if the crying doesn't stop, and the child is unable to calm down. This gives the parent enough relief from guilt to be able to dislodge their child's grip, walk away, and let you handle the situation.

More often than not, once those crying kiddos enter your beautiful classroom and look around in awe, fewer tears fall. As they put away their backpacks in their special spot and begin to experience all you have purposefully planned for them, tears slowly subside. Soon they are busily engaged in the day's activities and laughing with their new best friend they met that day.

To relieve those worried parents, I'd suggest shooting a quick text at recess or lunch to let them know all is fine. The time you invest in those first weeks partnering with families is the best tip I can give you for starting off on the right foot for a successful school year. This includes sending a note of welcome to students and their families prior to meeting them, inviting parents in for a chat, and sending home positive communication about each student. Such preparation will assist in smoothing any ripples that might occur later in the year.

Classroom Corner

*   What is your biggest challenge in preparing for a new school year? Organizing materials? Meeting parents? Setting classroom guidelines? Getting comfortable with students? Partnering with the home? Something else?
*   What strategies will you adopt in advance to turn that challenge into a home run for you and your students?

Teacher's Toolbelt

Want a smooth-running classroom that other teachers eye with envy and want to know, "How does she do it?" It starts with being proactive and establishing clear procedures and positive expectations with your students on day one.

Greet each student at the door as they arrive and connect names on the roster with faces. Tell each student to look for their assigned seat, get their notebook and pencil out, and begin the bellwork posted on the board. That way as you greet students, chaos won't reign.

After all students are in their seats, state your expectations for the year, including classroom rules and treating each other with respect. Explain how they will enter the classroom and proceed from activity to activity, whether within your classroom or down the school halls.

Usher students out into the hallway and do a trial run on entering the classroom. If students don't enter as you request, state your expectations again. Repeat that entrance until it's done the way you want it done. Yes, this might feel a little hardcore on day one. But this is do-or-die time. Waffle now and the most enterprising of your students will give running the classroom a shot later.

WHISPER
AND THEY'LL PAY ATTENTION.

It's all a matter of paying attention, being awake in the present moment.
The magic in this world seems to work in whispers.
CHARLES DE LINT

"It's one of those days," a teacher-friend confided. "My class is so chatty. How am I supposed to teach when they won't listen?"

Any teacher can empathize. We all have those days where the noise level is on overload from the instant students walk through the door. There's nothing like nonstop-talking students to make a teacher want to throw in the towel. You wonder if you're really accomplishing anything with your efforts. Are you being heard at all?

Actually, you are being heard, loud and clear. In fact, your students' chattiness is merely an outward sign of your need for assistance in managing a classroom. If you don't manage the herd with high efficiency and effectiveness, your students will step into the gap to try to manage you and their classmates. But they're not nearly as good at it as you can be, if given the right strategies. Worse, they create chaos in their wake.

You can return yourself to the driver's seat with this simple strategy. The next time your class is getting loud, don't raise your voice. Instead, whisper. It'll work every time to literally quiet the classroom waters. Guaranteed.

Why does this work?

First, most humans can't stand to see your lips moving and not know what you said. Their curiosity takes over. A little angst also might kick in: *Did I miss something? Is there a quiz tomorrow? No? Yes?*

Second, despite all evidence to the contrary, your students want in their hearts to please you. You are their teacher, and they want a relationship with you. You spend a significant amount of time with them every day. In fact, they might see you more than they do their parent(s) and siblings. That means what you say is important to them. They really do want to hear you.

But here's the problem. Students need time to move and to engage socially. Countless studies show that movement improves attention, reduces behavior and mental health issues, and creates more meaningful, engaging classes.[4] Educating the whole child is important. Our students are becoming adults, with likes, dislikes, feelings, and experiences that influence how they learn. Providing opportunities to interact and work alongside their peers in a positive way helps create future leaders.

If you don't plan times for students to engage in targeted interaction, they will engineer their own times, and chaos will reign. There are many techniques to stop the volume before it ramps up. The "Teacher's Toolbelt" ideas throughout this book will put you in the driver's seat so your classroom car is less likely to go out of control.

Will chattiness still occur? Yes, from time to time, because kids are human beings as well as learners. But when those times occur, you've already got the secret in your back pocket: *just whisper.* Whispering works wonders. Use it liberally. We do.

Classroom Corner

*   What time of the school day might work best for you to try out the whisper? Why? Brainstorm ways to proactively approach this typically loud time in your classroom.

*   How are you incorporating social engagement needs into your classroom routines?

Teacher's Toolbelt

Have you considered providing a purpose to any movement in the classroom? For example, it's time to line up for lunch. Ask the class to quietly skip-count by nines as they gather their lunches and get in line.

Maybe you've been learning a poem. Have your students recite it and be ready to go to the next activity by the time you get to the end. Or what about incorporating the high-five shuffle? You ask a question and have students move around the room and high-five a partner to create a pair of students. Now you can give another question for discussion while the students are in pairs and, if needed, tell the class to shuffle again and find another partner.

For younger students, you can ignite imagination by having them move like they are on the moon or jump like a kangaroo to the carpet. You wouldn't want to sit in your seat all day, would you? Neither do your students. Movement is healthy and necessary. It gets the blood flowing and allows for a healthy change of pace.

USE TECHNOLOGY AS A CLASSROOM SUPPLEMENT, NOT YOUR REPLACEMENT.

Technology is just a tool. In terms of getting the kids working together and motivating them, the teacher is most important.
BILL GATES

What role do you think technology should play in the classroom? Here's what some teachers we surveyed said:

* "Call me 'old school,' but I don't really think I need it to teach."

* "Let's be honest. Showing an educational video when you have a heap of tests to correct helps you catch up on the pile while the students get to learn something new."

* "I think kids spend way too much time on tech, and they don't need to get more of it in the classroom."

* "I use tech in the classroom—after all, we're in the 21st century, not the Middle Ages—but only if I feel it will enhance what I'm teaching, not replace what I should be teaching."

* "We didn't have tech classes when I was getting my teaching degree. Keeping up with rapidly changing technology is overwhelming, so I prefer using other methods. I want kids to learn how to relate to humans, not just computers or their cell phone."

Ask any teacher about technology, and you'll likely encounter one of two opposing schools of thought. It's either "Don't use it at all" or "Open the floodgates. The more, the merrier."

Wise teachers fall somewhere in the middle. They realize that technology is part of our everyday lives, and it's not going to go away. Ask any two-year-old to find YouTube on their iPad, and they do it with ease. There's also plenty of opportunity for screen time at home if parents deem that's appropriate.

But wise teachers know that technology is a tool, and that tools can be used for beneficial or detrimental purposes. For example, technology has prompted leaps in science, medicine, and AI. Its information fosters curiosity, exploration, provides platforms for communication, and opens new avenues for creativity.[5]

However, technology also has noted negative effects, including psychological, social, and physical ones.[6] It can lead to decreased physical activity, sleep deprivation, struggling with face-to-face communication, and addiction.[7]

The CDC reports that children ages 8-10 spend an average of six hours per day in front of a screen. Kids ages 11-14 spend an average of nine hours on a screen, and youth ages 15-18 spend an average of seven and a half hours a day in front of a screen.[8] With screen time that high, you wonder where school, friends, family, and life beyond technology can fit in. For some, technology has become an electronic babysitter that replaces in-person relationships and conversations.

However, not using or referring to technology at all is comparable to a tortoise hiding under a rock because it's afraid of a new environment. It might be more comfortable there, but the tortoise doesn't get anywhere, and you won't either, especially relationally with tech-savvy students. The question then is not, "What role should technology play in the classroom?" but, "How much technology use is a good thing?"

THE WAY OF THE TEACHER

It's our personal opinion, backed by numerous studies, that time in the classroom needs to be rich, filled with living ideas and deep discussions. Sure, an occasional video or other technology can be used to supplement the concept but never as the sole tool of learning. Teaching through videos and relying too heavily on technology can create passive students. It can short-circuit the teacher-student relationship.

Learning needs to be hands-on and energetic. It should provide a wealth of opportunities for students to wonder, be curious, and ask questions. The environment should allow for plenty of collaboration and prompt exploration that leads to the ability to think critically.

Used wisely and sparingly, technology can enhance that broad range of learning and also promote relationships and understanding in the classroom. If your students experience school through all their senses, their learning will be much more memorable.

Always keep your eye on the prize of technology's advantages and steer clear of its detriments. You'll be more energized in your teaching, and your students will be engaged participants in their own learning journey.

Classroom Corner

* Think about how you use technology in your classroom. How might you use technology in one area to the fullest of its benefits, without its detriments?

* What is your school's philosophy on technology? In what way(s) does it align or not align with your personal views? How might you address that discrepancy?

Teacher's Toolbelt

Recently I did a teacher training on the use of wonder in the classroom and the profound impact it has on students' learning. To introduce the concept, I played a one-minute video clip featuring Niagara Falls. While the video was playing, teachers were asked to write down five "I wonder…" questions that they had about Niagara Falls. After that one minute ended, teachers shared one question from their list without repeating what another teacher shared. Using a short video in such a way helps set the stage for the learning to follow.

Did you know that you can take virtual tours of nearly anything? You can tour the Taj Mahal or the Pyramids in Egypt. You can observe art in museums and constellations in the sky. With a simple click, you can travel anywhere.

However, here's the difference. You can play a 30-minute video on volcanoes to *replace* your instruction. Or you can play a dramatic one-minute video clip of a volcano erupting and *use it as a springboard* for the learning that is to come. A wise teacher uses technology to her advantage but never replaces her teaching with technology.

HIGHLIGHT SMALL-GROUP INSTRUCTION AND INTERACTION.

The art of teaching is the art of assisting discovery.
MARK VAN DOREN

We bet that if you were asked about student engagement in your classroom, you would hope it would be fairly high. Are we right? Well, here are some facts you need to know:

* The larger the group, the lower the engagement.
* The smaller the group, the higher the engagement.

Research overwhelmingly shows the following benefits of small groups in education:

* Whoever is doing the talking is doing the thinking.
* Students retain more information in small group settings.
* Teachers provide more timely feedback to students.
* Students learn how to collaborate and share strategies and observations.
* Teachers develop deeper relationships with students.
* Student engagement and participation skyrocket.

Who wouldn't want those benefits?

Small-group instruction is a masterful way to teach. And the benefits we listed are only a few of them. Teachers are also able to collect more data to inform their instruction, identify and encourage differing learning styles, and build rich relationships with their students…all in one fell swoop.

Small groups allow students to take ownership of their own learning. They learn how to collaborate and share strategies and observations. Small groups provide a safe place to ask questions that more cautious students may not dare risk asking in a large group setting.

So, let me ask you: how often during the day are you teaching to a whole group versus pulling a group of students to you to teach? Is your room set up for small-group instruction? How you've arranged your room conveys your belief about how students learn best. Are students' desks in pods to encourage small group interaction? Or in traditionally straight rows, emphasizing individual learning and focusing on you as lecturer?

As a professional educator you understand that all students are different. They have varying needs, abilities, and learning styles. Small groups are a great way to accommodate those needs by differentiating instruction.

Let's say you have five students who struggle with landing a specific math concept. Another four are getting their feet wet in it, and it's starting to make sense. Another five or so are rock-stars on the concept, and the other students in the class fall somewhere between. How would you handle that situation?

You could choose traditional math instruction that is textbook driven, direct instruction from you. It's whole-group instruction driven by worksheets and continual drilling of the concepts. There's no differentiation between students who have varying learning styles. All lessons are taught the same way. You provide step-by-step instruction that is the same instruction you gave to last year's class. Math is treated as a separate subject not related to other subjects.

Or you could choose Guided Math Groups. Explained simply, guided math is when teachers organize and facilitate flexible, fluid, small-group-learning opportunities for three to six students. These opportunities support and scaffold various levels of understanding while using new strategies, models, and a variety of materials. The math is well planned with student needs in mind. It promotes self-education and autonomy. The groups are flexible. The lesson and the teacher provide differentiation for varying learning styles. The teacher is able to continuously assess what the students know. Math is applied to the real world and connects to other subjects.

Which approach sounds more interesting to you and more fun for the students? Hands-down, it's the small-group approach. In a recent Professional Development Day at one of our schools, teachers shared the benefits and value of small-group instruction. Here are some of their insights:

* Allowing students to work independently builds trust with your class.
* The instruction is targeted and the content accessible to all students.
* Students are up and moving, are less restless, and more engaged.
* Sharing in small groups feels safer and builds confidence.
* Small groups encourage peer-to-peer learning and respect students as learners.
* Students have increased buy-in and take responsibility for their learning.
* It's great for gathering data and re-teaching concepts.

* Students build relationships with others that they may not have otherwise.
* Teachers can better attend to students' social-emotional needs.
* It's fun!

Who wouldn't want all that? Why not try out a small group this week? Or expand your use of small groups? You have nothing to lose and everything to gain.

Classroom Corner

* If you could implement one small-group experience into your classroom, which one would you choose? Why?
* Write the names of your students on a sheet of lined paper. How might establishing small groups assist with meeting the varying needs, abilities, and learning styles of each of your students? Next to each name write one specific benefit for that student.

Teacher's Toolbelt

Small-group instruction encourages peer-to-peer learning, deeper relationships, and respects students as individuals and learners. It builds confidence in asking questions and solving problems. It actively engages students' interests and makes them partners in their own learning.

Ready to implement small groups more effectively into your classroom? Try these tips.

1. Organize and plan well for each small group. For example, when grading a math test, make notes of which students missed certain concepts. Use your data to formulate groups of students with

similar abilities. Reteach the concept to specific groups until the content is mastered.

2. To meet varied learning styles, provide small-group instruction that includes visuals, manipulatives, oral direction, tactile resources, and movement.

3. Teach the expectations for learning in small groups and practice the routine until students understand the expectations. For example, students need to know what they can do independently without requiring your supervision. Students from other groups should not interrupt your "teacher table" to ask a question since you have already equipped them with what to do. They may discuss the question among themselves or appoint a group member to be a scribe and make a note of that question for when you do come to their table.

4. Keep student groups fluid to increase learning and build thinking and relational skills.

SET A PLAN AND EXPECTATIONS FOR PARENT-TEACHER CONFERENCES.

No school can work well for children if parents and teachers do not act in partnership on behalf of the children's interests.
DOROTHY H. COHEN

If you've been a teacher for at least a year, you already have your share of parent-teacher conference stories and lessons learned the hard way.

Like the first-year teacher who hadn't yet mastered how to move long-winded parents out the door. She soon had a long line of toe-tapping other parents, and some conferences had to be rescheduled. But that teacher was a smart cookie who didn't crumble. For the next conference, she used an old-fashioned alarm clock with a "you can't miss it" ring to end the session. She allowed a minute to usher the parents out the door with a few positive words and another minute to usher the new parents in the door. Her sessions ran like clockwork, while growing her relationship with the parents.

Or like the teacher who literally had to insert himself between two partners who acted like prizefighters sparring in the ring the minute they walked in his classroom door. As he said later, "There wasn't a class on that at my teacher college." After that, he set ground rules for all his conferences. If there were two adults, while one talked, the other listened. Neither was allowed to interrupt. The goal was a respectful, beneficial, and targeted dialogue.

Both teachers learned valuable lessons about setting parameters at parent-teacher conferences. How can you provide an environment conducive to problem-solving and maximize your time together?

Start by making your classroom a welcoming environment. As parents enter, greet them warmly. Then give a roadmap for the conference. If there are two adults, say, "I have a question for both of you. I'll ask one of you first, and we'll hear that person out for two minutes with no interruptions. Then I'll ask the other one, and we'll hear that person out for two minutes with no interruptions. Which of the two of you would like to go first?"

Having the two other adults in the room make that small decision together is a stepping stone to resolution. They might be warring partners, but they have to agree at least on who will go first. In this case, let's say Dad opts to go first.

Then you launch the question. "What concerns, if any, do you have about Max?"

Each adult gets their time on the speaking platform. You don't control what he or she says. Instead, you act like a gym monitor with a whistle around his neck. You follow your own rules. You don't allow any interruptions, and that includes you. So you focus on Dad and hear him out. You nod and use body language to show that you understand what he is saying.

Then you turn to Mom and say, "Now I want to hear your perceptions. I realize they might be very different." It is her turn to shine. No interruptions are allowed from Dad, or your figurative whistle comes out and you repeat the rules. The rules keep that conference from becoming a heated free-for-all.

In a short time frame, both feel heard and understood. Then you can move on to a mutual resolution of little Max's issues. His homework is sloppy. He gives it a lick and a holler. Both parents agree at least on one thing: neither understands why he does that.

But we do because we know a thing or two about families and understand the differences in kids in the same family. Max is the youngest of three, the baby brother of two older sisters. The two girls have a three-year and a five-year start on him in life. They bring home accolades and grades that make their parents go "Oooh." He can't compete with that. No wonder he isn't doing jack-diddly on his homework. Instead, he's focused on doing life differently: being the best at being the worst at school.

When you point that out to the parents, you'll look like a genius.

If you want to know more, read *The Birth Order Book: Why You Are the Way You Are,* by yours truly. It'll tell you why firstborns are often stressed, why middleborns are more secretive, why you respond the way you do to certain students, and much, much more.

Classroom Corner

* How do you view parents and guardians? As partners in their child's learning, hurdles to leap over, or something else? How does that view influence the way you feel about parent-teacher conferences and perform during them?

* We stated earlier that partnering with your students' families to start the year right includes: 1) setting the roadmap; 2) informing them about good things happening with their child; and 3) encouraging mutual problem-solving of any issues that might come up during the school year. How could doing those three things form easy talking points for you at parent-teacher

conferences? Would you switch the order of those points? If so, how, and why?

Teacher's Toolbelt

How can you best engineer a successful parent-teacher conference? Following is our "Top 10 Tip List" to knock your time together out of the ballpark.

1. Prepare a sample packet of student work ahead of time to demonstrate each child's abilities.
2. Post your conference schedule outside your door. Set a timer and stay within its parameters. You can always arrange for an additional meeting if needed.
3. Show that you know their child by sharing a funny or encouraging story.
4. Listen, listen, and listen.
5. Be positive and offer sincere encouragement.
6. Share specific strengths you see in their child. Give examples.
7. Select one area of growth. Discuss how you and the parent or guardian can partner together to implement it.
8. Write down concerns so you can follow up on them later.
9. Ask for feedback on your class, classroom, and homework load.
10. Leave on a good note, thanking them for their input and taking time for the meeting.

EXPECT THE BEST, GET THE BEST.

Optimism research teaches us that we should expect the best and have a contingency plan for the worst.
PAUL DOLAN

I had just found out that the kid with the worst reputation in all of school was on my classroom list. That morning I walked the hallways, catching empathetic headshakes and a few relieved "I'm glad it's not me" exhales from other teachers. I smiled and walked on confidently.

You see, I knew a secret: you get what you expect. Expect the worst, and you'll likely get the worst. But expect the best and you might be very, very surprised. If you don't get that best, well then, a little reality and relational discipline can help nudge things in a beneficial direction.

I didn't talk to that student's former teachers. I didn't read the files on the chaos he had allegedly caused. I simply prepared to meet him like every other child with warm enthusiasm and a friendly, "I'm looking forward to a great year together."

When other parents started to tell me stories about that "bad" student, I said kindly, "Every year is a fresh start, and I think every child deserves that chance, don't you?" The naysayers had nothing to say after that.

When a student told me the first day of class, "Nobody likes him," I looked her straight in the eye. "I like him," I said, "and he is now a student in my class. You are a student in my class. I will not allow anyone to talk negatively about any of my students, including him or you." The messenger got the message.

From day one I tackled the challenge of getting to know him. I worked to form a respectful relationship starting with the basics: his likes, dislikes, and interests. As he received positive attention, his attitude and responses to his classmates started to change. Their attitudes toward him started to change. Where vicious gossip had reigned, smiles emerged and even a hand or two of friendship. By the end of the second month, the girl who had said she didn't like him was offering him a sharpened pencil from her well-organized stash.

Indeed, such miracles can happen in your classroom. They start with you. If others complain about a student, don't play the gossip game. Instead, expect the best. *Like* the student. Show your acceptance and good attitude with your words and actions. Engage him as an individual and include him as part of the group.

Maybe you notice that student wears a Charlotte Hornets T-shirt a lot. You might not know anything about the NBA, but you need to find a key to enter his heart. Finding common ground is a wonderful way to do that. A two-minute Google search of the Charlotte Hornets is all you need.

The next day you can share an observation, statistic, or interesting fact about the basketball team. Ask him who his favorite player is or what he thinks of their mascot. You'll capture his attention, get dialogue flowing, and begin forming a connection.

Expecting the best works in other ways. It has a pass-along effect at school and at home. Here's what I mean. We often like to go to sporting events as a family. Before an upcoming football game, our daughter, Adeleine, asked if she could invite another classmate to come to the game with her.

"Of course!" we said. "Who do you want to invite?"

She told us the name, and it didn't ring a bell.

Being naturally curious, I said, "Tell us more about him. I haven't heard you talk about him before."

Adeline shared that he was a boy in her class whom others picked on. But she saw his good qualities and wanted to invite him to the game so that he knew that she saw his value. We were proud of Adeline and the initiative she was taking to care for a hurting classmate.

It's a simple thing, really. Expect the best of people and approach them that way. Look for their value instead of their flaws. See their future potential instead of where they are right now. However, few choose to invest the time or brainpower it takes to pursue the option of expecting the best. Why not be the first one to impact the life of a student in such a way…and see the resulting transformation for yourself?

When you lead, others will follow.

Classroom Corner

* How might you identify students who need a fresh start in your classroom? What social signs and behaviors from them or others might be clues?

* Brainstorm how to engage each of those students' interests. How might you best connect with them and win their cooperation?

Teacher's Toolbelt

Start a detachable page journal that allows for two pages (front and back) for each of your students. Label the first page of every two-page section with one of your student's names. Once a week during lunch or a brain break, jot down positive observations about each student on their own pages.

At the end of the first month, skim the journal. Which pages have the fewest notes? Likely, those are the students who need your positive attention the most. In the coming week, try hard to catch them doing something *good*, and then lavish on verbal and written encouragement. Evaluate your entries the same way at the end of each month.

For a meaningful end-of-the-year gift, add a few lines of encouragement on each student's journal page. Tuck the page inside an envelope with their name on it and hand out the envelopes individually with a smile as they walk out the door.

There's nothing like handwritten notes to do the heart good and prompt it to keep doing good.

WIN EVERY TIME WITH RELATIONAL DISCIPLINE.

The task of the modern educator is not to cut down jungles,
but to irrigate deserts.
C.S. LEWIS

When a student acts up, do you use *punishment* or *discipline?*

Punishment focuses on "I want to make you pay." It's served up with a good dollop of anger and revenge. It considers the *child* as the problem. A child who is punished learns nothing except how to better get away with that behavior next time. Resentment brews, and rebellion grows.

Discipline focuses on "I want to teach you what's right." It's served up with a calm attitude and unconditional love. It considers the *action or event* as a symptom of an issue the child may be struggling with and seeks to grow the whole child.

We believe in discipline the Leman Way. What's that, you ask? It's *relational discipline.* Not only does it work every single time for every single situation, it's a win-win for you and for that student in your charge. You see, if your student doesn't have a relationship with you, any discipline you try will be for naught. Kids only care what you think when they know that you care, believe in them, and are invested in them.

Let's say you have a student who's adept at picking fights. How can you halt this behavior? The answer is more complex than meets the eye. First, you must make sure you have identified the original fight-picker. Second, you must uncover the reason for that behavior.

Here's an example. Rae, a second-grader who typically didn't get into trouble, got caught kicking a male classmate where it counted. Upon investigation, the teacher discovered that Rae had put up with Brett smashing her desktop down on her hand for a full week before she took action. The reason Brett did it? He admitted he liked Rae and wanted her attention. Well, he got it but not the kind he expected.

What do all students want? Attention. If they can't get it in a positive way from affirmation for things they're good at, they'll get it in a negative way. They'll create havoc and alienate classmates in the process.

Some kids like Brett might be negative attention getters. Take, for instance, the physically small kid who picks on somebody big to start a fight and then runs away like a swift little bunny before consequences rain on his head. The one who gets in trouble is the bigger kid since he's the one who reacts to the provoking. Behind the scenes, classmates wish somebody would clean that small student's clock. That's especially true if they've been on the receiving end of the fight-starting and been called out for it by the teacher.

At the opposite end of the spectrum is the big guy who wants to show everybody how tough he is and that he's boss. This is the typical bully people think of. He also is an attention getter but for a different reason. Psychologically speaking, such children don't feel like they're worth anything so they create self-punishing behavior. Although they are punishing themselves, they use others as the instruments to carry out that punishment and incur their classmates' wrath.

It doesn't take a Ph.D. to figure out that such students often come from environments where they feel hurt by life. In the beginning all they wanted was attention and affirmation from those they love and trust most—parents or guardians. When they didn't receive it, their attention-getting behavior progressed into the negative territory of power. They began thinking, *If I become the big man on campus, no one can hurt me ever again.*

No matter where your student falls on the spectrum, using punishment will drive attention-getting behavior further into the power realm. Instead, proceed gently with relational discipline. Identify the original source of the chaos and pull that student aside privately. Psychologically disclose what you think is going on. "Now I might be wrong, but I think you're doing X because you crave attention/are afraid of getting hurt…"

Let silence reign while he processes your words. Often he'll look startled. *How did Teach know that?* Then he'll be embarrassed for being caught playing his game.

That's when you reaffirm his value. "But as your teacher, I don't see you like that." You point out the positives you see in him, and the session ends with that affirmation. There are no "If you do that again, I'll…" comments. Instead, you allow him to walk away dazed and confused. That's a good thing. He expected to be hammered. Instead you gave him a dose of psychological analysis, and you were right. He knows you saw through his antics to what's going on in his mind and heart.

To heighten the takeaway, you said he was good at something. He'll be processing those words all night. Don't be surprised if he arrives as a very different student tomorrow. There's nothing like a little relational discipline to set a wayward student on a lifetime path of beneficial learning.

Classroom Corner

* Reflect on problem-solving methods you've used. Which have produced good results?

* In what current situation might *relational discipline* be helpful? How could you best use it?

Teacher's Toolbelt

Relational discipline often requires a fresh perspective on an age-old problem. For example, have you ever had a "tapper" in your class? You know, the student who uses his pen, pencil, or whatever is on his desk to make that repetitive sound?

A *reaction* might be to say, "Whoever is tapping, please stop." Or, if you know the perpetrator, you might say, "Dean, how many times have I asked you to stop tapping your pencil? It's driving us crazy."

A *relational response* might be to say, "Dean, I love that rhythm you are tapping. I've been teaching for years, and I don't believe I've ever heard someone tap so fluently before. Would you show me at recess exactly how you do that? I really want to learn from the best in the business." That way, Dean gets the attention he wants but in a positive way. He is fully expecting your wrath, but a new relational twist makes the situation a win-win for both of you.

HOLD STUDENTS RESPONSIBLE AND ACCOUNTABLE FOR THEIR BENEFIT.

Mistakes are… Expected, Respected, Inspected, Corrected.
ANONYMOUS CLASSROOM DISPLAY BOARD

A teacher once asked me, "What do you do when one of your students clearly is having a bad day? Do you let it go unless the behavior is repeated the next day? Or do you take a hard-line approach so it won't happen again?"

My answer? You don't do either. You take the relational discipline approach, which lets reality play out and puts the ball of responsibility and accountability in that student's court. Then he gets the opportunity to choose whether he wants to go through the same scenario ever again.

If you want your students to be responsible and accountable, you start by giving them responsibility. Such responsibilities include paying attention in class, completing their assigned work, and participating as part of the classroom community. Then you hold them personally accountable for that responsibility.

If an eighth-grade student's attention wanders during class, you don't pull her aside and say, "I want to make sure you heard that there is going to be a quiz tomorrow. I can go over what will be on it again with you after school, if you wish." No. You let her sink or swim.

Yes, she may be woefully unprepared for that quiz. She might look like a deer in the headlights as she stares at that paper. But chances are good she's likely to listen much more closely the next time you give instructions. Now is the time for her to learn that lesson when the stakes are fairly low. Do you think that, in college, her professor will give her such slack and reminders? Or that her someday supervisor at work will?

A first-grade student refuses to do his part in cleaning up his own supplies after an art project. You take note but say nothing. During the next art project, he goes to get his bin of supplies, including a hardened paintbrush that was never washed. He wants a new brush.

You state calmly, "We don't have any other brushes. You'll need to figure out how to use that one."

That student spends all of his art time trying to clean his brush in the sink and misses the fun. Do you think he'll take better care of it next time? You bet.

As a teacher, one of your responsibilities should be going out to the curb with your students at the end of the school day. That helps you get to know your students, their parents, guardians, or drivers, whoever they are. If you are doing that, you already have a perfect set-up to handle any lack of responsibility or accountability. If not, today is the day to start.

Before you go out to that curb, write a personal note. You've already set up parents and guardians at the beginning of the year for using such notes as a problem-solving tool. You've explained that part of learning entails holding individuals responsible and accountable for their own actions. So parents have been prepped that receiving such a note might be a possibility.

Your note can be very succinct and go right to the issue:

Dear Ms. Smith,

Jonathan chose not to do any classwork today. He was uncooperative and also chose not to listen. Attached is the work he missed in class that will need to be completed tonight.

You write the note to mom, dad, grandma, or that student's guardian. When you get to the car, you hand the note to the child in full view of the guardian. Then you say to that adult, "Jonathan has a note for you." Jonathan himself has to hand his guardian the note.

Here's why that simple little action is so important. Students who misbehave have it easy as they stand outside the field of life and observe as parents and teachers talk *about* them and problem-solve *for* them. But bring them into the middle of it all and make *them* the focus of attention, and that misbehavior starts turning around. It's all about responsibility and accountability.

Yes, I am the guy who came up with the book title *Making Children Mind without Losing Yours.* But the truth is, you can't really *make* children mind. However, you sure can set the circumstances right so a student thinks, *Hey, I'm money ahead if I roll with the program here.*

Classroom Corner

* Comedian Lily Tomlin once said, "I like a teacher who gives you something to take home to think about besides homework." How might those words encourage and empower you in the classroom?

* What could you do this week to highlight the concept of responsibility in the classroom? Add quotes about responsibility on the board? Start a "Let's Do It Together" list? How might you more effectively hold students accountable for their individual and communal responsibilities?

Teacher's Toolbelt

Missing homework tends to be a common occurrence in schools. Teachers have the same chat with these offenders every day. "Where's your homework?" they ask. But nothing seems to change.

If you want things to change, place the ball of responsibility in the student's court. When it's time for recess, lunch, or any other extra activity, simply hand the student his homework to finish. If you're consistent in your follow-through, such action will usually do the trick in no time. The key is not to make a fuss over the missing homework. Simply remain calm and matter of fact. Break time and fun time comes after homework is done.

Once students see that they will be held responsible for their work, they'll tend to make a better decision next time. If not, keep on with that same routine. For repeat occurrences, investigate to make sure that the student knows how to do the work, has a place to do homework at home, and that no other circumstances impede his ability to get the work done. *(Since homework is a big issue, more on this in the next Principle.)*

Above all, be relational. Be consistent, firm, and fair. Students will come around.

ADDRESS THE ROOT CAUSE OF THE BEHAVIOR.

Beneath every behavior there is a feeling. And beneath every feeling there is a need. When we meet that need rather than focus on the behavior, we begin to deal with the cause, not the symptom.
Anonymous

A student turns in incomplete homework or none at all. How can you turn that behavior around? You must discover the reason behind it by staying on the trail like Sherlock Holmes.

After a week into the school year, you should know your student well enough to discern whether the behavior is a simple lack of responsibility or something else is going on. If it's a responsibility issue, the fix is simple. What we call "reality discipline" kicks in. The child experiences the natural consequences of his decision. And don't be fooled. *Not* making a decision *is* making a decision not to do something.

The formula for reality discipline is easy to follow: Let reality be the teacher. B doesn't happen until A is completed. If he didn't turn in homework today, he uses his brain break or recess to complete it and misses getting to do what he wanted to do. Most often you only have to use this formula once before a student realizes, *Okay, I see how this works. If I don't do X, then life won't move on.*

A few students are more hard-core. They want to test you to see if you say what you mean and mean what you say. Here's their thinking: *I'll ride out this little wave, and Teach will let me off the hook because he'll get busy elsewhere.*

But reality discipline is a little like fishing. Hook a fish, and it'll try to throw the hook out of its mouth by leaping out of the water and thrashing around. Expect that fish-out-of-water syndrome with some students. They'll come thrashing wildly out of that situation with a rebellious "You can't make me," "But I don't want to," or "There's no point to homework" comment or two.

Such thrashing will especially occur if you've caved in the past. Now that you're smarter, and practicing reality and relational discipline like you're learning about in this book, you know you have to keep tension on the line to land that fish. Stay calm. Slowly, steadily reel that slippery fish in with another round or two of reality discipline.

But here's the catch: you have to be 100 percent consistent in your behavior. Follow the plan nine times out of 10, and you're back to square one. Never, ever let that fish off the line or it'll be tough to catch it again. Your students need to know you mean business.

However, if you sense something deeper is going on, pull that student aside privately for a sensitive conversation. "I notice that you are having difficulty completing and turning in your homework. Perhaps something is going on in your life that would help me understand why. If so, I'd like to help."

Perhaps the student doesn't get any support at home with school work. He might return to an empty house or have a lot of chores to do, including taking care of younger siblings. By the time he's done, he's exhausted and has little time or brain-space left to do homework.

If such is the case, think creatively about providing opportunities for that student to finish his work while at school. Maybe consider shortening an assignment. Does the paper really have to be 1,500 words? Or would 750 suffice to teach the same lesson? Meet the student where he is and support him as best you can.

The student may also be struggling with high parental expectations. Is he a perfectionist? Afraid to fail? Is he not naturally good at the subject where he's missing homework? If he has two neuroscientists as parents, or one authoritarian parent determined to run the show and lower the boom if he doesn't make the grade, no wonder that student doesn't turn in his homework even if he completed it. Since he can never measure up to those expectations, procrastination has become his go-to coping mechanism.

If so, it's time for a parent-teacher conference. Sometimes teachers need to be gentle family counselors as well as tenacious student advocates. Most high-expectation parents have no idea how much pressure their children feel every day to rise to those expectations. We can tell you numerous stories of families transformed by that simple information.

No matter the reason for the incomplete homework, you must address the root of the issue to change the behavior. Kids won't stop misbehaving on their own. They need a relationship with you, a good dose of reality discipline, and always, always, a listening ear.

Classroom Corner

* What behavior do you need to tackle in the classroom? What steps will you take to keep that fish on the line?
* If a student struggles with something else going on, how might you adapt assignments to fulfill what she needs to learn?

Teacher's Toolbelt

Did you know that teachers make an average of 1,500 decisions a day?[9] No wonder you go home exhausted. Some decisions are high impact; some are low impact. Some are easy; some are tough.

Anything concerning a student's well-being, whether emotional, social, behavioral, or academic, needs your attention. Hopefully you have support systems such as social workers and a school psychologist to lighten your load.

Some students come to school to learn because they are loved at home. Others come to school to be loved and aren't able to learn until they feel the classroom is a safe place. Keep those realities in mind as you navigate each student's need.

TREAT TEACHING AS A CONTACT SPORT.

I facilitate thinking. I engage minds. I listen to questions.
I encourage risk. I support struggle. I cultivate dreams. I learn every day.
I TEACH.
Jo Grubbs

I remember vividly the day I pulled through a drive-thru during the COVID-19 pandemic and saw a colorful sign promoting a contactless pay app. The pandemic created a whole new vocabulary for the field of education such as *contactless, distant learning, asynchronous instruction,* and *social distancing.* We were encouraged to mask up and stay six feet apart.

Wow. We certainly learned a lesson or two about how students learn best and the optimal conditions for successful learning and instruction during that time. We learned, in fact, that *teaching is a contact sport.* Students crave relationships, including close contact with peers and their teachers, physical participation in extracurriculars, and in-person instruction.

No technology, as smartly as you use it, can replace a warm greeting at the classroom door, an empathetic glance at the end of a difficult day, or an enthusiastic, in-person "Well done. That must feel good to work so hard to accomplish that and see great results." No matter where you teach, the following five tips will help you take advantage of and maximize your in-person time in the classroom:

THE WAY OF THE TEACHER

1. *Keep students always in your line of sight.* This allows you to closely observe student behavior at all times and provide support or redirection. It helps students engage in the daily routine. Continual awareness of student expressions also flags for you which of your students struggles with the concepts you are teaching. You can then engineer small groups accordingly to target any re-teaching.

2. *Stay mobile in the classroom.* Move around the room and students are more likely to pay attention. Close proximity allows a teacher to see if students are disengaged from the learning and to help redirect that behavior swiftly without drawing class attention to the student and risking peer embarrassment. A short pause by a student's desk will tell them, "I see you. It's time to get back on track."

3. *Win your students' cooperation.* Invest in getting to know them and their interests. For example, you overhear two students talking about their weekend. One mentions she spent time riding her horse. You use that information later to ask about the type of horse she rides, her horse's name, and the lessons she is taking. Being interested in what your students are interested in builds a strong classroom community. It takes such a short time but reaps huge dividends.

4. *Encourage sharing of perspectives and ideas.* Take advantage of small groups to facilitate sharing of those who are more introspective. Such sharing also stretches student horizons. It showcases that others can be different and think differently from you, yet you can find common ground.

5. *Highlight community, courtesy, respect, and a "we're all in this together" mantra.* Such intentionality will increase your students' knowledge that what impacts one of them impacts all of them and that their actions influence the lives of others.

After the pandemic, education has struggled to get back to normal. But is there really such a thing as normal? A good history teacher would tell us we must learn from the past. If we don't, we are bound to repeat it. Years have now passed since the national school shutdown caused by the pandemic. But rarely a week goes by that I don't hear someone still blaming low student achievement on the pandemic instead of taking positive steps to move forward in that area.

How *do* we move forward? Frankly we need to stop making excuses for what isn't working and plunge wholeheartedly into what we know works. We need to take the bull by the horns, jump back into the race, get behind the wheel and drive, and get the train back on track.

Those are a lot of word pictures all clumped together to drive home the message: we need to be immediate, intentional, and proactive for things to change. Students, above all, need a relationship with you. They need to know you care. They need to know that they can make mistakes and still have your unconditional acceptance. They need your belief in them. They need you to stretch their horizons of possibility.

All those things can take place with you being proactive and intentional in the classroom. That's why we need to treat teaching as a contact sport. The stakes are too high and the risk too great to stay idle. You might be the only one in your students' lives who broadens their thinking, listens to their questions, encourages curiosity, supports them in their struggles, and helps them cultivate their dreams. With your assistance, who knows the places they can go and the things they'll be able to accomplish?

Classroom Corner

*   Which one of the five tips do you think is most important to a successful classroom? Why?

* How might using all five tips grow your relationship with your students? Give an example.

Teacher's Toolbelt

When teachers spend the majority of the day at the front of the room, where the whiteboard is front and center, student engagement plummets. Students will find nearly anything in their desk or pencil box more exciting than what's going on in class. What would change if there wasn't a clear front of your room? A new trend in education is to "defront the classroom."

If you notice students are more engaged with a paperclip than with your lesson, change things up a bit. Get students moving and talking. Evaluate your voice level, instruction, and pace of teaching. All those will impact student engagement. A carefully designed lesson will create the learning atmosphere you desire and make for a more enjoyable day of teaching.

STUDENT RELATIONS

One looks back with appreciation to the brilliant teachers,
but with gratitude to those who touched our human feelings.
The curriculum is so much necessary raw material,
but warmth is a vital element for the growing plant
and for the soul of the child.
CARL JUNG

DON'T TREAT THEM THE SAME.

Fair isn't everyone getting the same thing.
Fair is everybody getting what they need
in order to be successful.
RAMONA POPE

Remember when you were in kindergarten, and one of your art projects as a class was to draw and then color an apple with crayons? Did your apple look like anyone else's? No. Each apple created by you and your classmates was unique.

Well, the students in your class are unique too. If they were fruits, they wouldn't all be apples. Some might be oranges, pineapples, dragon fruit, lemons, kiwi, or kumquats. You'd have, in fact, a whole basket of fruits.

But when you think about each student, which of the four descriptions fits that individual best?

> #1: A natural leader and perfectionist. Logical, technical, well-organized, conscientious, a good reader, and a list-maker. Takes life seriously and doesn't like surprises.

> #2: Self-motivated, a voracious reader, and a high achiever. Thinks in black and white and uses *always* and *never* a lot. Completes every project thoroughly, expects a lot out of herself, and doesn't like to fail.

#3: Independent, sometimes secretive, and a diplomatic mediator. Goes out of the way to avoid conflicts and often compromises to keep the waters of life smooth. Deeply loyal to friends.

#4: Affectionate, charismatic, and a people person. Enjoys the limelight and surprises. Engages easily with strangers. Makes classmates laugh.

Students you placed in #1 are likely either firstborns or the first of their gender in the family. Those in #2 are probably only children in their family. Those in #3 are assumably middleborns. Those in #4 are no doubt lastborns.

How can I be so confident? After studying birth order for years, I've seen these descriptions play out over and over. Birth order isn't an exact science, because not all characteristics fit every person in that birth order. Variables such as the number of years between kids, gender, physical, emotional, or mental differences, adoption, death, blended families, and a critical-eyed parent can change that birth order (for more, see *The Birth Order Book*).

We already discussed basic birth order traits and how they influence you and your responses to students in Principle #3. Now let's look at how they impact your students. What do your students most need from you?

Firstborns and onlies need to know exactly what the rules are. They need things laid out from A to Z and feel uncomfortable when they aren't. Since they are already perfectionists and hardest on themselves, they take any criticism deeply to heart. They don't appreciate others trying to "improve" on their work. They like to figure things out for themselves, so give them assistance only when they ask for it. Yes, they're responsible, but don't always appoint them the leader of their small group. Firstborns and onlies respond better to adult company than children of any other birth order and often crave it…especially if they have younger siblings who tend to garner attention at home.

Middleborns often avoid sharing how they really feel and think, so intentionally ask for their opinion and allow them to make choices. Set aside times for the two of you to talk. It's important to give that kind of time to each of your students, but a middle child is least likely to insist on his fair share. Make sure that middle children feel they have a unique role to play in your classroom. Listen carefully to their answers, explanations, and takes on certain situations. Their desire to avoid conflict and not make waves may get in the way of the real facts of a situation. You may have to say gently, "You're not in trouble. I only want to know what really happened and how you feel about it."

Lastborns need to learn to do their fair share of responsibilities. They often wind up with little to do on group projects because they're masters of passing the buck. Because they're seen at home as so little and "helpless" that other family members decide it's easier to do a task themselves, lastborns may try the same approach with their classmates. If that happens, kindly call that baby's bluff. It's important they pull their weight to learn responsibility. Since they often think, *Nothing I do is important,* they also need to feel achievement. Because they love the limelight, a smile and a "Good job!" can keep that lastborn performing to the best of his ability.

See how different the birth orders are? That's why treating everyone equally isn't the best *modus operandi* in the classroom. There's a wide gulf between treating every child with equal love and respect and treating them "the same."

Classroom Corner

* Reflect on the different needs of the birth orders. Which one need would you say is most important for firstborns and onlies? For middleborns? For lastborns? Why?

* Ask your students, "If you were a fruit, what kind of fruit would you be? Why?" Not only will it be a fun assignment, whether written or shared in a small group, but it will give you insight into how your students think and feel.

Teacher's Toolbelt

If you are teaching a child how to read and she has trouble with a word, how would you proceed depending on her birth order? *(No peeking below until you've made your own assessment.)*

> *Firstborn or only:* Don't jump in with a correction. Give her time to sound out the word on her own. She's a "do it by self" kind of girl.

> *Middleborn:* Let her attempt it on her own. If she still struggles, say, "Why don't we sound it out together?" Middleborns value social interaction and time an adult chooses to spend with them.

> *Lastborn:* Don't fall for doing any of her work. She will tend to like to be read to instead of doing the reading. But when she learns, she'll feel a big sense of accomplishment.

WANT THEM TO TALK?
SHUT UP AND LISTEN.

Most people do not listen with the intent to understand;
they listen with the intent to reply.
STEPHEN R. COVEY

If you really want a student to talk, shut up and listen. Really, it's that easy, but it's counter intuitive for most of us adults.

After all, we've lived through more life experiences and can offer long-term perspective. So our gut might be to say seemingly helpful things such as:

* "I'm sure it will get better."

* "Are you sure you're not imagining it?"

* "It'll be okay. Don't worry about it."

* "Really, it's not that big of a deal."

Such statements are intended to calm the emotional tsunami so the child can be more logical and help problem-solve the current situation. However, such attempts will backfire. Statements like those actually shut down children (especially teens) because they see you as uncaring and clueless about the impact the event is having on them.

If you want your students to talk to you, here are three top considerations that need to be engrained in the way you relate to your students.

First, *realize feelings aren't right or wrong.* They're just feelings. You don't like others telling you how you should feel. Why would you do that to your student?

Second, *don't judge or minimize the drama.* When a student risks sharing with you something that is bothering him, keep your mouth shut. Behind all those emotions and words is the core of how he feels about himself and his world. To assist effectively, you need to understand that core.

Third, *engage actively.* Set aside any work you're doing. Listen to her words. Observe the emotion that flashes across her face and read her tense forearms. Do you see fear? Insecurity? Anger? Body language and facial expressions are as important as the spewing of words.

Here's something else to think about. When a student is brave enough to share with you, she's saying, "I trust you with my most secret thoughts and feelings." So pat yourself on the back. You're already doing something right relationally to garner such a move on her part.

Once you've got those considerations firmly in mind, it's time to proceed to the next level with these strategies for conversation.

Offer a short statement. "I can tell you've had a rough day. If and when you want to talk about it, I'm all ears." You don't press. You simply invite and wait. No one wants to be forced to share. Students will share when they're ready and only when they're ready. Exercise your superpower of waiting. They will share eventually, and when they do, you'll learn far more about them, their home, and their stresses than you could ever imagine.

Say, "Tell me more about that." It's a great door opener into stimulating conversation, even for teens typically as mute as Egyptian sphinxes. It also allows the student the opportunity to explain what he is thinking and why he is thinking that way. Those five words bypass the curveballs students tend to throw your way (and they can throw some doozies). Instead of being stuck in a react-to-immediate-information loop, give yourself the time and opportunity to gather more information before you choose how to respond.

Be realistic about your role. Children really don't want you to solve their problems for them. They want you to be a listening board. Only by learning how to wrestle with problems and issues in a healthy manner will they become well-balanced, problem-solving adults.

Solicit their opinions. Many children hate being asked inane questions such as, "So…how was your weekend?" But asking an opinion is different. Most people *love* to give their opinions. Doing so makes a participant feel valued and respected because he can contribute to the group.

For example, a 13-year-old in your class is fascinated by tortoises. He wrote his science paper on them. You are thinking about getting a class pet you can keep from year to year. Why not ask that tortoise expert for his opinion on different breeds? It will save you a lot of research and have him grinning ear to ear that you believed he is competent and capable to help you.

Twenty years down the road, when he is a lauded herpetologist, we bet he'll remember that moment he was able to contribute his knowledge for the group's benefit.

Classroom Corner

* Think back to your growing-up years. What advice did a well-intended adult give that you weren't ready to hear? How did you interpret it? What do you wish they would have said or done instead?

* Reflect on this quote by Carl W. Buehner: "They may forget what you said but they will not forget how you made them feel." Why not post it where you can see it every day as a reminder that what you do matters, and matters greatly?

Teacher's Toolbelt

Most schools have something like a "Career Day," where professionals come and speak about what they do in their respective vocations. Why not also invite parent experts into your class? Hearing about their experiences is a powerful way to encourage young minds to think about their futures.

However, we often overlook the young people who sit in our classes day after day. Don't forget they too are experts, with something valuable and knowledgeable to share. For example, how many times have you been stuck on a tech issue and turned to a techy problem-solver student to assist you? He does it with ease and gets you back on track.

Allow students an opportunity to share what they know and do well. Maybe the budding artist provides a painting to hang in your classroom or the musician writes a class song. You could have a future photographer, dancer, athlete, or doctor in your midst. Invest in what they're interested in. It will bring fun to your classroom too.

UNDERSTAND WHAT THEY WANT MOST.

Building relationships with students is by far the most important thing a teacher can do. Without a solid foundation and relationships built on trust and respect, no quality learning will happen.

Larry Ferlazzo

Let's debunk a major myth right now. It's *not* your job as a teacher to make your students happy. Nor is it your job to make their parents happy. Feeling good is a temporary thing. It's based on feelings, and those change from moment to moment.

But it *is* your job to understand what children want most and to provide that for them every day in your classroom. If that sounds hard or overwhelming, we assure you it's not. All you need is to know, understand, and employ the ABCs every day in the classroom.

These ABCs might not be the ones you're used to. They're not the letters that are often colorfully posted in a kindergarten room. Instead, they are the three pillars of self-worth for every human being. All your students need them in liberal doses.

Let's briefly look at each one.

A = Acceptance. Your students crave your approval and will live up to your expectations. Allow them to do things on their own. It might mean struggling, making mistakes, and sometimes failing. That's not only okay, but good. By supporting their abilities to tackle whatever it is head-on, you are saying, "Go for it. This might be rough going for a while, but I know you can do it. I believe in you." Your students will fly high for a long time on that kind of encouraging wind.

B = Belonging. Everybody needs to belong somewhere. But children will never feel like they belong unless they can contribute and pull their own weight. Don't do for any child what he can do for himself. Working hard for something establishes true self-worth. Your students need to be able to think, *Wow, look at that. I really did it. I worked hard, and did it all by myself.* Anyone can feel good about getting something they want. However, true self-worth is established when a person works hard for that something he wants, earns that something, and can truly call it his own.

C = Competence. Want your students to gain psychological muscle to power through whatever comes their way at school, much less in life? Then give them responsibility. If they follow through with that responsibility, say, "Great job. I can tell you worked hard to study for that test. Bet that made you feel good inside."

What about when an outcome isn't good? That's also a success. The student has learned what didn't work. Next time he can choose to do things differently for a different outcome. A case in point: it took Thomas Edison 1,000 unsuccessful attempts before he created the first light bulb.[10]

Every child longs for your acceptance, your unconditional love and approval.

Every child needs to belong somewhere. Will it be in your classroom?

Every child needs to be seen as competent. Do you want to empower your student? Then give him responsibility and hold him accountable. His confidence in himself and in his problem-solving ability will both increase.

Classroom Corner

* How are you intentionally building the ABC pillars of self-worth into daily activities in your classroom? Into relationships with your students?

* Want to improve your students' self-worth and problem-solving skills? Try out these time-tested ways that will also boost your relationship.

  1. Identify positive traits you observe and tell students often.
  2. Compliment their uniqueness.
  3. Thank them for what they do to make your class a caring community.

They may not seem to be listening at that moment. However, be assured your words will return when they need affirmation most.

Teacher's Toolbelt

Recently I spoke to a teacher who struggled to connect to her newly assigned classroom. I popped in to watch her teach for a few minutes and quickly discovered a well-structured, highly organized, neat, and pretty classroom. But something was missing.

The teacher was robotic and steeped in her routines, taking little visible interest in her students. They were called on by their classroom assigned number and lined up by their number. Even the discussion sticks in the jar on her desk had numbers. Nothing in the classroom reflected her students' individuality.

In our chat after school, she asked what I thought might be hindering her relationships with students. After complimenting her organization skills, I kindly and gently shared my observations and that her classroom didn't feel the way I believed she wanted it to. She had focused on the aesthetics of the room instead of the beautiful people inside its four walls.

We talked through simple changes in routine tasks such as greeting students by name as they enter the room, writing their names on sticks in the jar on her desk, and taking attendance by having students respond with an answer to a fun question instead of "here." These easy ways begin relationship building and show you care for your students as individuals.

What do you do when a student is absent for multiple days, out sick, hospitalized, or dealing with other issues? Do you communicate to absent students that they are missed? Do you take the time to call the home and check on how your student is doing? Do you send encouraging messages from your class? A class video message to bring a little joy and a smile? All these ideas send a message: *You are missed, cared for, and your school community is thinking of you.*

Students desire to feel that they belong in your classroom. Do your students know and feel they are a special, valuable part of the classroom? Little changes in words and actions go a long way toward building relationships and showing you care...personally.

UNDERSTAND WHAT THEY FEAR MOST.

Teachers help find strengths, wipe away tears,
overpower demons, and conquer fears.
UNKNOWN

Did you know every student sitting in your classroom faces a trio of fears? These fears drive their reactions to all that happens. This includes their relationships, what they share in class, how they handle test-tasking, and much more. These fears intensify as children become teens and magnify actions that can harm themselves or others. However, when you know and understand the fears, you can help students navigate them by taking advantage of powerful, easy-to-use solutions already at your disposal.

What are these fears?

Fear #1: Rejection and failure. No one wants to be rejected or feel like a failure. We all want to be liked, accepted, and good at something. But for older children, these cravings can trump anything else, including logic and long-term thinking, because of the intense drive to be part of a group. Worse, when liking is based on who's highest on that day's food chain, rejection is hard to escape. Failure is also a very real option when doing anything for the first time.

The solution? Unconditional love and acceptance. Learning how to handle rejection and failure positively is critical to ultimate success. You can help by listening, empathizing, and then offering perspective. "I can understand why that bothers you. And of course it hurts. But you know what? When I look at you, I see someone with a kind heart, who helps others and doesn't give up on them. Remember when (and you share a story about them)? It makes me smile and think how lucky I am to have you in my class."

That student can't help but exit your classroom with his very own smile.

Fear #2: Uncertainty and loneliness. Roller-coaster peer relationships and changing body parts is enough to create tumult. And no child would willingly sign up for the teen years if given the option to bow out. But add uncertainty from a home environment or a perceived inadequacy, and negative emotions skyrocket. There's nothing worse than having a horrible day, needing to talk, and having no one to talk to.

The solution? Stability and presence. Your rock-solid, positive presence is critical. Students need to know they are safe. They are respected individuals in a community run by a healthy authority. The rules are known by all and unchanging.

Give students an open invitation to talk with you, but do not press. If a student seems troubled, pull her aside in private. Say quietly, "I notice you seem to be having a hard time lately. If you ever want to talk, I'm here and ready to listen." She will talk…when she's ready.

Fear #3: Bullying and insecurity. Anything different about you, or the simple fact you're breathing next to an insecure individual fighting to ensure he's top dog, can paint a target on your back. With the ease and anonymity of social media, there are few, if any, consequences to gossip-spreading. Anyone can say anything about anyone at any time and share it at the speed of light, where it will float around endlessly in the electronic universe. No wonder students live in fear of being socially ostracized.

Most children are insecure in some way. Bullies don't act on their own and need a posse. Shunning, cliques, and name-calling abound in the survival-of-the-fittest jungle. Every day kids wonder, *Who will be today's target? I hope it's not me.*

The solution? A balanced perspective and a "we're all in this together" guarantee. Bad things do happen and people can be mean. Both are facts of life. You must be proactive in setting a respectful tone. Share a time you were targeted by meanness or bullying and how you felt about that situation. Point out that students who pick on others behave like they do because they don't feel good about themselves. Taking someone else down makes that student temporarily feel important. There's nothing like uncomfortable truth to pre-empt bully or mean behavior. In an eat-or-be-eaten jungle, nobody wants to look insecure.

With your assistance, the trio of fears won't be as scary.

Classroom Corner

* Which of the three fears is easiest for you to navigate? Which is most difficult? Why?

* To combat the fears, what rules could you post in the classroom? Some ideas are:

> Treat others as you'd like to be treated.
> Be a friend to everyone.
> We'll all in this together.
> *Add your own....*

Teacher's Toolbelt

The concepts of bullying and meanness may be similar in that they both cause injury to others. But don't confuse the two. *Bullying* is the repeated targeting and relentless pursuit of another individual. It must always be taken seriously with administrative support, swift consequences, and communication to the homes of any students involved. *Meanness* is saying or doing something negative one time or occasionally and requires a simpler plan of attitude-action adjustment.

When a student is mean, let the recipient privately vent to you without judgment. Say, "Tell me more" to get the full story from their perspective. After the story is complete, count to 10. Allow silence to reign. Then say, "No wonder you're upset. I'd be upset too if that happened to me. So what do you plan to do about it?" That prompt encourages a transition from victim venting to workable next steps.

Such a session must occur before you gather the two for a private face-to-face. Give each side a minute to share without interruption. Then move to next steps. The two must brainstorm and work out the solutions themselves. Such work generates understanding of others, solidifies the concept of consequences, and prompts beneficial behavior.

Why does this work? No child wants to be embarrassed, especially in front of a peer. There's nothing like having to look a person you've wronged in the eye and say, "I'm sorry for X," to make you realize, *Yikes, I really was a knucklehead*. Receiving a peer apology minimizes emotional damage, boosts self-worth, fine-tunes relational-conflict skills, and allows life to move on.

I.D. AND ASSIST HURTING KIDS.

If kids come to educators and teachers from strong, healthy, functioning families, it makes our job easier. If they do not… it makes our job more important.

BARBARA COLORSE

In today's unpredictable world, hurt is inevitable. Intense peer pressure and competition, betrayal by supposed friends, derogatory comments on social media, and family changes and transitions can further increase a child's uncertainty. Add the steady diet of headlines highlighting school shootings, war, environmental changes, and ethnic, gender, and gang violence, and it's no wonder children and teens face significant trauma.

How can you help? First, *you can identify hurting students through their behaviors, changes in behavior, and physical or emotional signs.* Perhaps a typically chatty student goes silent or a student slumps in his chair, unable to focus on school work. Maybe a student goes out of her way not to pass another student's desk or drags her feet at packing her backpack at the end of the day. You might see unexplained bruises or cuts or a lack of caring about hygiene. All those and more are signs of a hurting student who needs your attention.

Second, *you need to earn the right to enter your students' inner worlds.* Four simple principles will help you develop a relationship. Only by earning their trust can you assist them in developing the strength and resilience required to handle adversity in a healthy manner. Such assistance will also include partnering with the family, the school counselor, and potentially others outside the school if and when necessary.

What are these principles?

Acknowledge that the hurt exists. If it's clear an elephant is sitting in your classroom, you wouldn't ignore it, would you? Ignoring that a hurt exists won't make it disappear. The simple words, "I sense that you are hurting, and I'd like to help. If you ever want to talk about it...or cry...or want some company, I'm here," will speak volumes about your support. Just make sure you say those words privately and respectfully.

Allow them to express feelings without judgment. Feelings are not right or wrong. They are simply what your student feels and as real to her as a fact. If you want her to talk, be an engaged listener. Listen without judgment or offering solutions. Focus solely on her. Nod or say, "I hear you," from time to time to show your understanding. Let her pour out her feelings and thoughts however she wishes. Neither adult logic nor long-term perspective stated now will win your student's heart. If you don't win her heart, you won't win her ears later when she's ready to listen.

Encourage them to strategize next steps. After your engaged listening, show empathy, understanding, and that you heard her by making a comment like this: "What a rough day. I'd be upset too."

A light dawns in your student's eyes. Someone believes her and understands her. She sighs in relief. She's no longer alone in this situation.

Now that you've got her attention, you apply the teachable moment.

"But you know what? In the midst of that very personal attack, you didn't throw mean words back. That reveals so much about your character. I'm really proud of you. So, what's your next move?"

You see, your role is not to solve the situation, but to encourage your students to strategize next steps. Taking action themselves will strengthen them in this and other life storms, improve their resilience, and short-circuit a victim mentality. When should you intervene by calling the shots?

If any child is physically, mentally, or emotionally in danger, there's no question: immediately get the appropriate adults involved.

Be a realistic champion. "What happened to you was really tough, no doubt about it," you say. "But I believe in you. You're strong and life-smart. You can rise above this situation." No, life isn't always a Disneyland experience. But your belief in your student as a capable, growing individual means more than you will ever know.

If you focus on developing a supportive relationship with your students, you'll help them navigate difficult experiences with a lot less drama (and we teachers know all about that). You'll also instill competence and a positive attitude toward future challenges.

Classroom Corner

* Ask yourself, *Which individual(s) in my class might be hurting today?*
* How might you listen to and specifically engage with those students?

Teacher's Toolbox

Adam, a top striker on your school's soccer team, is targeted with malicious gossip by a team member who wants his position. Adam is typically even-keeled but now looks like a thundercloud. What should you do?

> *Option 1.* Sit tight and wait until the thundercloud is ready to talk, even though you already know what happened.

> *Option 2.* Present the evidence and publicly call out the malicious team member on the gossip.

> *Option 3.* Listen with engagement, empathize, and then walk alongside Adam as he strategizes next steps.

Combining options 1 and 3 is a winning combination to instill in Adam positive problem-solving, competence, and resilience. It will also likely take care of the peer-group situation, rather than you acting as the hammer of retribution.

Adam's wise teacher chose options 1 and 3. The result? The next day Adam gave his coach the heads-up and asked if he could say a few words to his team members before practice. His speech was delivered with a calm, steely gaze. "I'm really disappointed in you guys. If you don't like something I've done, tell me straight. Don't start a rumor about me and hurt an innocent girl's reputation. She deserves better than that, and I want you to stop." He nodded at the coach. "Thanks, Coach. Now let's hit the field." He turned his back and walked away, leaving behind a group of head-hanging-low athletes…especially one.

Sometimes a little peer embarrassment is exactly what's needed as a life lesson.

ADDRESS THE UNIQUE CHILD, NOT A LABEL.

*If a child can't learn the way we teach,
maybe we should teach the way they learn.*
IGNACIO ESTRADA

Someone once said, "Every child is gifted. They just unwrap their packages at different times." We love that unknown author quote because it's true. But we'd add to it that they also unwrap their packages in different ways unique to each child.

Diagnostic labels assist us as educators in defining the issues that certain students might face. They help us identify ways these students might learn better than traditional methods. But we do ourselves and those children a disservice if we focus on the label instead of the child. We limit our ability to recognize that student's unique potential and to present her with educational challenges that will grow that potential.

During my senior year at North Park University in Chicago, I had a masterful professor, Nancy Berggren, who not only taught the Special Education courses but also had a huge heart for her students. I still remember her saying that a child's diagnosis should never come before the child or define the child. She explained, "You don't ever say, 'Autistic student' or 'ADHD student.' They are people, first and foremost." She trained us to think of such children as "a student who has autism" or "a student who is being treated for ADHD." Adjusting your wording in such a way can influence your perspective on the children in your classroom who are part of the Special Education program.

Each child is a unique creation, with a distinctive collection of skills and bents that helps to inform their learning style. "I have a student who cannot sit still," a teacher told me recently. "I ask him all day long to stay in his seat, but he wanders around the room. It's distracting for me and his classmates. What can I do? How can I help him?"

All students learn in different ways. Some students need to move in order to remember. The term for that is *kinesthetic learning*. How can you help? A purposeful seating chart can provide your student with the space he needs to move. Try moving his seat to the side or back of the classroom where he can stand to work or walk in the back of the room without blocking your view of his classmates.

There are also some tools you can try if the student needs to sit. Try a Velcro strip under his desk that he can feel or recommend a wiggle seat. A bouncy band on his chair for his feet, a fidget tool, or a weighted lap belt can also be helpful. A parent volunteer once made a few students in my class each a felt lap belt filled with rice. The students could put such a belt on their laps and enjoy rubbing the felt texture. It helped them stay in their seats when they wanted to sit.

It's also valuable to have a chat with your student who is a kinesthetic learner and understand what would help him learn best. Ask him if he'd like to move to the side or back so he can stand or move whenever he wants. Ask him if certain textures are calming for him to touch. He will appreciate your interest and accommodation of his needs. Part of building a wonderful relationship with each of your students is getting to know each of their learning styles.

If you have a student who would benefit from your school's special education program, ask questions so you understand your role in the process. That role can also change sometimes, depending on school policies and vacillating funding for the Special Education program. If students in your class have a 504 Plan or Individualized Education

Plan (IEP), know that those are legally binding documents. It's critically important that you know exactly what is in the student's plan and that you follow the list of required accommodations in your classroom. Both plans provide support for the student to be successful at school. Partnering with your school's Special Education team will help you understand how to modify the curriculum and what additional supports are needed in your classroom.

Classroom Corner

* Do you know the specific needs of each of your students? Which ones have a 504 or an IEP? Can you articulate what each plan requires of you? Seek out your Special Education department if you need more guidance on what to do.

* As a teacher, remember your role is never to diagnose. Never tell a parent that their child has ADHD, autism, Tourette Syndrome, or any other diagnosis. You are not a doctor. If you have concerns, start with your Special Education department and follow your school's guidelines.

Teacher's Toolbelt

If you have a student with special needs, it's vital you are in close communication with the family, school nurse, and Special Education department. I always met with those three groups as students were evaluated or diagnosed. The family especially is a rich resource (as they are with *any* classroom concern) because they know their child best.

Ask parents, "What works at home when Ben has a hard time focusing on his homework or a task?" Listen carefully. Ask their opinion and suggestions about your game plan. If they want you to try something unorthodox, say you are willing to try anything that might help for two weeks. Then you'd like to meet again and reevaluate how it's working.

Allow parents to freely communicate with you if the student is having a bad day, if medications changed, or if behaviors are improving at home due to a new strategy. Most of all, always advocate for these students. Never allow any teasing or ostracizing. All students belong in your school and in your class.

SEEK OUT AND ENGAGE WITH LONER STUDENTS.

In case no one told you today... hello, good morning, you belong here, you're doing great, I believe in you.
PRESCHOOL BULLETIN, ASHLEY PERALES

A teacher once asked me, "I have a student who is very quiet. He doesn't seem to make friends or want to engage with anyone. Should I be worried? Should I prompt him to be more social?"

Truth is, I don't know whether that teacher should be worried or not because I have not interacted with that student. I don't know his background or anything else about him other than those few descriptors. However, simply being quiet is not a danger sign unless it's combined with other factors such as a straight A student retreating from life and failing to turn in his homework. In fact, here are some realities to consider.

A lot of people have excelled in life, including as professionals and family contributors, who by their nature are quiet. In fact, their happiest moments are when they are alone because that's their brainstorm and regrouping time. There's nothing wrong with that.

I have spoken with talented architects, engineers, and other highly productive people who have basically told me, "It would be great if you could keep people away from me so I can work on this project." If a student is quiet, that may simply be his make-and-model. Not everyone needs to be the center of a party happening 24/7. In fact, our world would likely be in more trouble if every individual were social.

However, if your spidey senses are tingling, telling you something more might be going on, do some careful observation and research. Note the student's demeanor as he enters your classroom, leaves your classroom, and interacts with others in-between. Does he retreat into a turtle shell? Can you sense discouragement, resentment, or rage?

If the student has a social media account that is public, check it out. What is its tone? Do any words state or imply a threat to his or others' safety? If so, he needs immediate intervention by those who have been trained to do so at school. Parents or guardians need to be called in to be a part of that intervention.

The best thing you can do is share your concerns with the person in authority over you at school. Not only is it the right thing to do, but, to put it bluntly, you're covering yourself legally. We're all too familiar with events where students have tragically taken the lives of others or ended their own. Media headlines often describe such individuals as quiet loners. However, behind the scenes, it's likely that life has gone terribly amiss for those students. That includes abuse, bullying, betrayal, and abandonment by adults who should have protected them when they were at their most vulnerable.

If your student is simply more introspective by nature, then, no, you cannot "prompt him to be more social." The old saying is true: You can lead a horse to water, but you cannot make him drink. You can't make someone be more social, either.

You can, however, provide an environment that is warm and welcoming to give him the opportunity to be so. You can broaden small-group opportunities to help him get to know other classmates better. You can seek out his opinions. You can engage one-on-one with that student through his interests. You can get to know his family better. Showing curiosity about him as an individual boosts you to a very significant person in the life of an introspective student.

Still waters often do run deep. And they can make for fascinating individuals to know.

Classroom Corner

* Which students in your class tend to be on the quiet side? In what way(s) have you attempted to engage their interests? What has worked? What has not worked?

* What new techniques might you try to engage with such students? Brainstorm a list. Why not try one idea out this week? You might be surprised what fun things you learn. And the smile you receive from that student? It will fill your entire day with sunshine.

Teacher's Toolbelt

Every teacher should be aware of warning signs that a student needs assistance beyond what is available in the classroom. Such SOS signs include:

* Extreme withdrawal, lack of engagement with any activity, seeming to care about nothing.

* High levels of anxiety, perfectionism, depression, or obsessive-compulsive tendencies.

* Extreme discouragements and comments such as, "What's the use? Life's not worth living."

* Symptoms of addiction, such as glazed eyes, inability to concentrate, alcohol on breath, etc.

* Unexplainable bruising or cuts or suddenly wearing long sleeves in 90-degree weather.

* Secretive behavior, such as skipping meals or making excuses to eat in secret, quickly changing a phone or laptop screen, or unwillingness to share their texting partner.

* Excessive focus on healthy food, counting calories, or body image. This includes expressing disgust, shame, or guilt about eating, regularly visiting the restroom after eating, and frequent body checks in mirrors. Eating disorders such as bulimia nervosa or anorexia nervosa can impact females or males, but females have a five times higher rate of such disorders occurring.[11]

* Seething rage that boils up and causes intent to or the action of a verbal outburst or physical blows at others.

* Making sexually explicit comments or acting in a way that should be beyond their age-applicable knowledge.

Yes, children, and especially teens, can be mercurial in their moods. However, the above signs must be taken seriously. Students should be addressed gently and kindly accompanied to the school counselor's office.

Once there, the school processes of partnering with the parent and professional psychologists should take over in assisting the student. However, you should keep tabs on the process and the student. In short, as a mandatory reporter and guardian of your students' safety, always report any concerns to administration.

NEVER DO WHAT A CHILD SHOULD DO FOR HIMSELF.

The teacher's task is to initiate the learning process and then get out of the way.
JOHN WARREN

A kindergartener refuses to hang up his backpack on his assigned hook. Nothing you say seems to work. He wants you to do it for him. There are three types of teachers. Which type you are will determine your response.

Authoritarian "my way or the highway" teachers run highly organized, no-nonsense classrooms with precision and overabundant rules. They major on knowing what's best without engaging personally. They bark out orders. They lay down the law with threats like, "Class, if you don't behave, you're all going to lose your recess." When the infraction occurs, they drill the point home with a twist of revenge: "I told you you'd lose your recess if you didn't behave. Well, now you've lost it. Instead, you will each write an essay on what you did wrong."

Permissive "what else can I do for you?" teachers want things to run smoothly and for all students to be happy. Their rules are more like suggestions since they change depending on the situation and students involved. They always want to know what others think and feel and major on everybody getting along. They are overly relational since approval from students and parents is very important to them. If anyone is unhappy, that teacher feels she is doing something wrong. If students complain about a pop quiz, the teacher says, "Well, we don't really have to have a quiz. Why don't we just review the information instead to make sure you all know it?"

Both *authoritarian* and *permissive* teachers miss a critical foundation for teaching responsibility and accountability: students learn best what they learn for themselves. Such teachers may seem like they're opposites, but both decide everything for the child. The child doesn't have to do anything. The path is already paved. Children only need to concede and do what the authoritarian teacher says. They can easily wiggle out of anything they don't feel like doing with the permissive teacher.

How can you introduce responsibility and solidify accountability? You should never do for a child what he should do for himself. That's the way of the *authoritative* teacher.

Such a teacher is always in healthy authority, establishing respectful rules that never change. All are expected to treat others in the way they'd wish to be treated. Authoritative teachers intentionally seek to know each student to uniquely motivate that individual to the best of her abilities. They have high expectations and let reality do the teaching if students drop the ball of responsibility.

How would each teacher handle that kindergartener's lack of responsibility?

The authoritarian would bark out an order: "You are going to hang up your backpack, and you're going to hang it up *now.*"

The permissive teacher would say, "Oh, that's okay, honey, I'll do it for you today. Don't worry about it." And then she'll do it for him every day because that kid has her number.

The authoritative teacher would allow the child to make his own decision and then live with the consequences. How does such authority work? You don't say anything. That puppy stays right where he drops it. Eventually that kindergartener will need to find something in that backpack so he can be like the other kids. You simply wait for the teachable moment.

It comes at lunch time for that all-day kindergarten. In the students' rush to get their lunches out of their backpacks, that backpack on the floor gets trampled en route by myriad little feet. The boy pulls out his lunch and it's a squished mess. Peanut butter and jelly with the crusts cut off doesn't look nearly as good when it's as flat as a pancake. He looks at all the other kids happily eating their lunches and takes only a few bites. His stomach growls during afternoon activities.

After school, you accompany the boy to the curb. You say to his mother, "Emilio has something to tell you." He himself is responsible to hand over the note that explains what happened.

The next day, guess who hangs up his backpack right away? Lesson learned. And you didn't have to say a thing.

As a bonus, here's a short course in psychology. Whoever invented the statement "The apple doesn't fall too far from the tree" had some great insight.

Either the tree is so authoritarian that the kid rebels. He refuses to do anything anybody tells him to do. That's a bad recipe for his success at school.

Or, at the other extreme, he has a parent who is too permissive and does everything for him. Therefore, he's expecting you to take over that special treatment. Hanging up his backpack is a test to see if you'll fall in line with what he expects. After all, everybody at home does things for him, so why shouldn't you?

It's time to show that things are done differently in your classroom. When you do, his parents or guardians might marvel at the changes they see and ask you about them. His future partner will also thank you down the road. See why authoritative teachers can change the world?

Classroom Corner

* Which of the three types of teachers are you? How did that style influence how you handled a difficult moment in the classroom?

* Replay that moment using the authoritative style. How might you ensure the child is held responsible and accountable for his own actions?

Teacher's Toolbelt

5 Key Things to Remember

1. Kids rise to the challenge if expectations are high, clear, and lack wiggle room for miscommunication.

2. Doing for children what they should do for themselves is not respectful.

3. Each child's best differs based on age, talents, and the activity.

4. Children don't need praise, which links their worth to what they do. They need encouragement, which emphasizes their growing character.

5. If you major on relationship and minor on everything else, you'll never go wrong.

ENTER THE TEEN ZONE WITH KNOWLEDGE AND EMPATHY.

Great teachers empathize with kids, respect them, and believe that each one has something special that can be built upon.
ANN LIEBERMAN

At the beginning of the school year, your students welcomed your thumbs-up of affirmation with childish enthusiasm. Now, six months later, you use the same gesture and the eye-rolls of "you're so out-of-touch" disdain abound. What happened in the interim?

You have entered the rapidly changing environment of the teen zone.

No doubt, middle school and high school are tumultuous years for teachers and for students. Many teens change moods more often than they change their undies. On any given day, friends come and friends go. Body parts and processes change. Emotions not only ebb and flow with peer tides but crash down like tsunami waves.

There's an innate desire to grow up, all while craving a simpler childlike world where any problems are fixed as soon as they occur. How else can you explain a beginning middle-schooler who throws words in your face like a cocky little banty rooster in the morning but after school wants a hug before he goes out the door? Or the silent-as-a-mountain high-schooler who stalls after class until her peers are gone so you'll notice her and ask what's bothering her?

With such a volatile internal world and a survival-of-the-fittest external world, your students need stability and a place of safety. They crave your support and encouraging presence. They want you to understand them even when they don't understand themselves. The teen years are transitional times in a swiftly expanding universe. How you approach four key factors can make or break your relationship with the teens in your care.

The first factor is *independence.* The teen zone is the nebulous area where your students are still children, craving your protection, safe boundaries, and guidance. On the other hand, they desire freedom and independence. That's why they don't welcome questions. In fact, they *hate* questions because they view them as a challenge to their developing authority.

It's not that they don't want to talk. Think of it this way: How would you feel if someone threw nonstop questions your way? Or demanded answers? Your students simply need to be approached in the right way. They will always welcome statements such as, "I'd love to know what you think about…" or, "Tell me more about that…."

Making such statements shows interest in what your student thinks. It encourages her next-step process. It also shows appreciation for her uniqueness despite her insecurity as a work-in-progress.

The second factor is *stress.* Body changes and mental development prompt significant pressure and tension. Teens tend to blow up as a way of releasing those feelings. A student who seems fine one moment may be orbiting the planet the next. What does that student need from you? A hefty dose of grace, a sizable helping of understanding, and a lavish tablespoon of second chances…the very same things you'd want if you made a mistake and feel a little embarrassed about it afterwards.

The third factor is *peer pressure and identity.* Fitting in with the peer group is extremely important for most teens. What other students think of them matters far more than they let on. The student who may seem to brush off an unkind comment will likely go home and cry at night in secret because of it. Even the teen who seems popular still works hard to fit in. She knows she might be unseated from the popularity throne the very next day.

Such volatility makes teens highly sensitive to any criticism. Small comments, a wayward look, or a perceived shunning or snub bother them greatly. Peer criticism is particularly devastating because of their intense desire to be accepted by the group. Any difference of clothing, body shape, background, or genes is highlighted and then can be picked on. Students never know when they will be "it"—the target for the day.

Kids will do absolutely anything to fit in with their peers. I ought to know. I did a lot of dumb-as-mud things since I craved the limelight. How can you help? You must be proactive, setting and following guidelines for a safe, mean-free and bully-free zone in your classroom. All students must be treated with respect and act respectfully. Any infractions also must be addressed immediately and respectfully.

The fourth factor is *privacy.* If teens want you to know something, they will tell you. If not, they will keep their mouths shut. No force of nature and no cajoling will open that mouth until they're ready. Be respectful. Grant them the same space you'd want if you were them.

Approach these four factors with ultra-sensitivity, and you're already on the road to a winning relationship.

Classroom Corner

* Think about your middle-school and high-school years. What's the most challenging moment that comes to mind? The most positive interaction you had with a teacher? How did those

moments impact your emotions, relationships, and the way you viewed school?

* Based on your interpretation of those events, how might you alter how you interact with the teens in your class now? Why?

Teacher's Toolbelt

"Empathy is a powerful tool that can help you better understand what's driving your students' behavior and find strategies to help," Amanda Morin says. "It can also help you connect and work through difficult moments together."[12]

Use the following acronym[13] to help you remember the key points of empathy.

E-Everybody needs somebody.

M-Model and mirror.

P-Put yourself in their shoes.

A-Ask if you can help.

T-Treat others the way you want to be treated.

H-Hurtful or helpful?

Y-You feel better, and they feel better.

Unknown

GIVE 'EM GRACE, JUST LIKE YOU'D WANT.

[Kids] don't remember what you try to teach them.
They remember what you are.
JIM HENSON

Think of that kid who keeps all the teachers on their toes, and that would be me. Little Kevin Leman earned quite the reputation at school. To this day, I both chuckle at my antics and feel bad for the teachers who had to put up with me.

You might have one of those students in your classroom right now. Patience is a virtue, your grandmother always told you. You're exercising a lot of it, at least most of the time, with that trouble-making student. But let's be honest. Sometimes you wish he were in someone else's class.

Yet you have no idea how much that student needs you. Dr. James Comer once said, "No significant learning can occur without a significant relationship."[14] Think of all the hours you spend with that child every week day. It may be the most time he spends with any adult. That means what you do, what you say, and the relationship you have is truly significant.

Remember the first few weeks of first grade, when you were so exhausted by 2:00 p.m. that you only wanted to go home? Lucas does. In a single afternoon, he got into a word fight with a classmate who broke his favorite red crayon and then fell asleep minutes later at his desk. But, miracle of miracles, he woke up snuggled warmly in a blanket in a corner of the classroom. The teacher had carried him there, tucked him in, and let him sleep during storytime.

Or remember middle school, when the only person you didn't want to be was yourself? Camilla does. A single zit was a Mount Vesuvius event and worth ditching a school day, except for her last and favorite class.

At the end of that class, the teacher approached Camilla privately. "I hear you've had quite a day," she said gently. "If there's anything you want to tell me, I'm all ears."

The teacher's kind tone prompted the out-pouring of Camilla's story, along with a few tears. Rather than sending her to the principal's office for ditching school, that wise teacher said, "Zits are rough, aren't they? Nobody likes them, but almost everyone gets them. I know something that might help…."

While Camilla was assembling her belongings at her locker, that teacher had a quick phone conversation with Camilla's dad. When he picked her up after school, he offered to get a treat on the way home. After getting ice cream at their favorite drive-thru, he said casually, "When I was a kid, I had a lot of pimples. Sometimes I just wanted to hide out and not go to school. This stuff worked for me. You can try it, if you'd like." He quietly handed over a tube of acne medication and then drove toward home. Nothing was said about her skipping school.

An incident that could have prompted days of lying about being sick in order to miss school or rebelling for getting hammered about skipping classes was transformed into a memory of love and support by the two most significant people in her life. One was a teacher who cared and went the extra mile on her student's behalf. The other was a father who grasped the stakes of zits for an adolescent.

What do these two real-life stories have in common? Both teachers extended grace to their students when those students did things they shouldn't have. We've highlighted in this book how important it is to teach your students responsibility and to hold them accountable for their actions. And that's critical.

But sometimes what's needed most is grace.

Grace is unmerited. It's unexpected. It's relational. It can change attitudes, turn situations into unforgettable life lessons, and pave the road toward transformation.

We all need a liberal dose of it.

Classroom Corner

* In your opinion, what are the biggest influences on your students that might exacerbate misbehavior? What could you do to mitigate these influences? Brainstorm some ideas.

* For encouragement, reflect on this quote by Justin Tarte: "Teachers who put relationships first don't just have students for one year; they have students who view them as 'their' teacher for life."

Teacher's Toolbelt

Every teacher needs a good dose of EGRS: Extra Grace Required Sometimes. Such thinking will help you deal proactively with whatever students might throw your way, while assisting in growing your relationship.

> *E = Expect the unexpected.* Anything can happen, so don't be blind-sided.

> *G = Give them room to grow and change.* Your students are still figuring out how life works and strategizing their roles. They need to struggle, make mistakes, and fail in the safety of your classroom. Give them guidance but ever so gently.

R = *Remember what your own growing-up years were like.* Be sensitive to what matters to them. Encourage them in private. Never embarrass them in front of their peers. Realize that social media pushes them to grow up faster than you had to.

S = *Sift through the real reason(s) for the misbehavior.* An action might feel directed straight as an arrow at you, but don't take that misbehavior personally. If you engage in a war of words, you'll never win. You'll both lose. You're the adult, so take the high road. Listen for what's behind the words before you act.

GOALS AND PERSPECTIVE

The future of the world is in my classroom today,
a future with the potential for good or bad…
Several future presidents are learning from me today;
so are the great writers of the next decades,
And so are all the so-called ordinary people
who will make the decisions in a democracy.
IVAN WELTON FITZWATER

VIEW STUDENTS AS LIFELONG LEARNERS.

Tell me, and I forget,
teach me, and I may remember,
involve me, and I learn.
BENJAMIN FRANKLIN

Ever had a student who seems to go out of her way to challenge you in front of the class? Who has to have the last word or the first word? Who needs to be the center of attention? If so, you're not alone. Not only is that situation frustrating for you, it's distracting for the other students.

But here's some fresh perspective. Instead of thinking of that student as a distraction or an annoyance, think about her as a learner. After all, that's what education is all about, isn't it? Learning and processing information so you can become your best self and contribute in a meaningful way to society.

The belief that students will live up to the expectations you set for them needs to be the foundation for all your decisions. We've already said to expect the best and you'll likely get the best. Then what's the best way to proceed with that learner?

Pull aside that student in private. In a calm tone, address her by name and say, "I've noticed that you are a deep thinker and that you ask good questions. I bet you like to do research. I'd love to hear more about what you think about (subject), and why it's so important to you. If you're willing to share, I'm all ears. Whether it's today, or any day, let me know, and you and I can set some time aside to talk. What you think on the issue is important to me. In fact, if you ever want to do more research, I'd be happy to set aside some time for you to share what you've learned with the rest of the class. They could benefit from what you're learning."

Turning a challenge into a relationship-building moment is a double bang for your buck. It will lessen the distractions for the class as a group and benefit you and your student. It will also likely introduce a new subject to your class that will prompt others to research and share their own topics. Such self-generated learning is priceless because it sets patterns for a lifetime.

After all, that student isn't only a kid. She is a developing adult with a tumult of thoughts, emotions, and a background of experiences that have greatly influenced her. There's no better way to say "I care" than to lend a listening ear and to treat her as a competent human being.

All that questioning and needing to be top dog might be a streak of rebellion, yes. It is also likely a desire for independence and a push to be noticed as a unique individual. But all those drives, if channeled in a healthy direction, have the power to beneficially impact the world someday. Who knows? You might have a future Einstein, Madame Curie, John D. Rockefeller, Oprah, or Bill Gates sitting right there in your classroom.

Think for a minute what it would be like to entertain the perspectives of a future entrepreneur in your classroom. You're likely to be thrown a few curve balls. That's why you never take on a student in front of your class. You're putting yourself in a no-win situation. You're outnumbered, and you'll lose every time.

Instead, wait for a teachable but private moment to discuss the behavior with your student. Such actions show your respect for her as a person, support her interests, and encourage her next-level thoughts. Imagine that student a decade or two down the road saying, "The first person to truly care about me and listen to what I was trying to say, even if I was doing it badly, was my teacher...."

That's why we say teaching is all about the 3 Rs: Relationship, Relationship, Relationship.

Classroom Corner

* William Glasser said that we remember "10% of what we read, 20% of what we hear, 30% of what we see, 50% of what we see and hear, 70% of what we discuss, 80% of what we experience, and 95% of what we teach to others." How might this quote influence the new methods you try in the classroom?

* Think about the style of learners you have in the classroom. How might you expand your teaching methods to more effectively steer each student onto a path of lifelong learning?

Teacher's Toolbelt

With every lesson you teach, there should be an "Exit Ticket." You need to ensure that your teaching of a particular concept is effective and that your students understand it. An Exit Ticket is a quick, low-stakes, formative assessment that guides the teacher on next steps. Do students truly understand the concept, or do they need a reteaching?

Examples of Exit Tickets include solving a problem on a small whiteboard, index card, scrap piece of paper, or a sticky note. How do you use them? Pose a question to the class and have students write their individual responses. Collect those responses and do a quick sort of students who got it correct and those who didn't. Then you can reteach the concept as needed to the entire class or select small groups of students.

Exit Tickets can be done either during the lesson, in the form of a quick check for understanding, or as an "out-the-door" activity. They also give students the opportunity to demonstrate that they've mastered or practiced a new skill, and that can feel good. Why not brainstorm some Exit Ticket ideas of your own?

REALIZE *WHY* IS MORE IMPORTANT THAN *WHAT*.

*In an effective classroom, students should not only know
what they are doing; they should also know why and how.*
HARRY WONG

How do you handle a negative behavior that happens not only once but multiple times?

"I've caught a student stealing from my desk and his classmates' desks several times," a teacher told me. "Sometimes he takes other kids' lunches. I've talked to him about stealing and why that is not a beneficial behavior, but items continue to randomly and mysteriously disappear from our classroom. I can't prove it is the same student taking all the items. But from his previous behavior, my guess is he's the one. Any tips on how to handle this situation?"

All behavior is purposive. In other words, there is a *why* behind that action. A student would not continue to steal unless that stealing fulfilled a need or gave him a gain in some way. You won't change the act or any future occurrence of it unless you find the reason behind the act.

Is that student stealing lunches or snacks because he is hungry, or is he stealing the lunches because they look better than his? Students who steal tend to do so for two reasons: the first is out of want and the second is out of need. How you handle the stealing depends on which of those two is the reason behind it.

When I was a Vice Principal, I worked closely with a young student who was caught stealing gum from his teacher's desk. During my investigation the student revealed to me that his parents didn't allow him to chew gum at home. He expressed how much he loved to chew gum.

In that case, a quick phone call home was all that was needed. The well-meaning parents had no idea their child was yearning for gum so badly. They were merely trying to protect his teeth from cavities. I partnered with them to allow him some sugar-free gum at school. The swiping of gum stopped. The student wrote a beautiful note to his teacher, who joyfully accepted his apology.

A similar situation developed with another student who stole pocket change from a teacher's purse. The student was merely attracted to shiny things and curious about coins since she had never seen them. The teacher partnered with the guardian to establish a "change jar" at home that the student had full access to and could play with any time she wanted. The stealing at school stopped.

Many behavioral situations can be simply solved by finding out the why and being creative. You can also read books to your class to address issues. For example, *Ricky Sticky Fingers* by Julia Cook is helpful in the case of stealing.[15] Books that teach specific virtues are wonderful tools to confront the myriad issues that arise in your classroom. Reading also leads to rich discussions that help solve many problems commonly faced by teachers. Even older students love stories.

Sometimes, though, behaviors are more complicated. That's when you must continue to slowly peel back the layers to get to the why. Never forget that there is always a *purpose* behind that behavior.

When situations happen that require discipline, first get the facts aligned and documented: *what* happened, *when* it happened, and *how* it happened. But you should not stop there. When you use relational discipline, you focus on the action as being detrimental to the student's own and others' well-being. You don't focus on the student himself as "bad." Without having a relationship with that student, you cannot ferret out the *why*. That student won't talk to you. Neither can you use that root cause of *why* to assist in creative problem-solving with the student and those at the student's home.

Every teacher has students who know how to push buttons and are really good at it. They like to see the classroom in chaos because it's entertaining. Other students live by default, without responsibility or accountability in their grid.

If students aren't receiving relational discipline and experiencing real-life consequences at home, the next-best place to learn those things is in the safety of your classroom. Right now is far better than later, when the consequences may be much greater. Stealing a sandwich is one thing. Stealing a car is another. For the good of all humankind, let the reality of consequences rain down.

Classroom Corner

* Review the past month in your classroom. What behaviors have been problematic? How have you handled them?
* How would you approach those behaviors now with relational discipline that gets to the *why*? With reality discipline that allows real-life consequences to occur? With creative problem-solving?

Teacher's Toolbelt

Teachers are always busy with time constraints, homework to grade, lesson plans to create, and the list goes on. Therefore, any temptation to place a Band-Aid over a problem as opposed to digging deeper is understandable. However, if we don't get to the *why*, that behavior will continue. You'll keep putting on a larger and larger Band-Aid and end up spinning your wheels because no change is happening.

That's why pursuing the *why* is vitally important. Behind every behavior, there is a story…a purpose that must be uncovered if you want the behavior to stop. Yes, the search for answers will take time. However, unless you can identify and yank out the root, that weed of purposive behavior will continue to grow.

PROVIDE THE ESSENTIAL VITAMINS.

*The dream begins… with a teacher who believes in you,
who tugs and pushes and leads you on to the next plateau,
sometimes poking you with a sharp stick called truth.*
DAN RATHER

Most people would agree vitamins are good for you. They have many health benefits, which include boosting your immune system, increasing energy levels, improving your mood, and reducing stress and anxiety, to name a few. But did you know that children also need other vitamins? And that you, as their teacher, are in a perfect position to give them what they need?

Let's take a look at what we call the "7 Essential Vitamins."

Vitamin A = Accountability. Do you hold your students responsible for their actions? Are they accountable to manage specific tasks and adhere to a timetable? Do they act with a good attitude as part of the classroom community and desire to contribute?

A late-bloomer will never bloom with too much hovering or watering from a permissive teacher or with too much smothering from an authoritarian. That student will merely become limp, unable to stand up under harsh conditions in the real world. An authoritative teacher gives students the opportunity to develop responsibility and accountability. He sets the roadmap, then backs off and lets students make their own choice: to take that opportunity or let it pass them by. That choice will have real-life consequences in the classroom and life outside that classroom. Whether students learn the hard or easy way will be solely up to them.

Vitamin B = Behavioral expectation. The old adage is true: you get what you expect. If you expect the best, you will likely get the best. If you prime your students by saying, "If you do…," followed by a threat, you'll get the worst because you've actually primed them to act up. Great expectations can make a great difference. Try them out in the classroom and see.

Vitamin C = Caring and cooperation. They don't care what you know, or what you think, or what you say until they know you care. Your relationship with your students and what role they perceive they have in your classroom has a great deal to do with their academic performance and social engagement as a community. The words you choose to say are critical for your students to want to listen. Caring means getting behind each student's eyes to glimpse how he views the world. It means having a heart-to-heart relationship that uniquely connects with that child.

Vitamin D = Discipline. Steve Jobs, the founder and CEO of Apple Computers, Inc., was born in 1955 to an unwed teenage girl and adopted by a working class family. Obviously Jobs was brilliant and talented, but he also learned to work hard at an early age. That discipline set him on a trajectory for life success and helped him get off the ground faster.

Assist a student with learning discipline and hard work, and you'll get him off the ground faster. It may not always be easy, but it's the right thing to do. Everyone makes mistakes. Everyone has flaws. But if your students have discipline, those mistakes and flaws can become life lessons. When bumps in the road inevitably come, those students won't be easily discouraged.

Vitamin E= Encouragement. There's a mountain of difference between *encouragement* and *praise,* and children can't be fooled. *Praise* makes empty, grandiose statements like, "You're just the best ever." The child knows that's not true. *Encouragement* uses statements like, "I love to see you dig into a project like that and finish it with great flair. And you figured that out all on your own. That has to feel great inside." A child who feels the internal success of knowing he did something well will always outshine in the long-term the child who is praised.

Vitamin N= No. Not everything is beneficial, nor is it healthy. Drawing clear guidelines and boundaries, rather than spouting rules, will help students explore their talents and potential within the safety of your classroom. Some teachers are afraid of saying no because they want their students to be happy.

However, a healthy child isn't always happy. If we paint life as an easy romp, we do our students a disservice because that's an illusion that won't hold up. Always saying yes fosters unhappy children who think the world revolves around them and owes them a favor.

Instead, we should set clear boundaries and pre-set responses if students step over a boundary. It's as simple as A + B = C and based on real-life consequences for that action. There are no threats, no reminders. You simply let reality do the talking, while your student does the learning.

Vitamin R = Respect. You should never allow disrespect in your classroom. All human beings are of equal value in God Almighty's eyes. Respect is a two-way street. You have to give it to get it.

In these 7 Essential Vitamins you'll see threads of concepts we've discussed throughout this book. Connect them, and you'll have a roadmap to meet your students' needs and boost their character growth.

Classroom Corner

* Which of the vitamins is hardest for you to give? Easiest for you to give? Why?

* Zig Ziglar once said, "You cannot tailor-make the situations in life, but you can tailor-make the attitudes to fit those situations." How could you provide the conditions where students have to hold up their end of the bargain with a good attitude?

Teacher's Toolbelt

As you consider these 7 Essential Vitamins, it's important to distribute them with consistency. Let your "Yes" be yes, and your "No" be no. Offer encouragement in regular, healthy, sincere doses. Avoid praise. Students have varied levels of family support, so your consistency in the classroom is a gift you can bestow daily with positive outcomes to follow.

MODEL, TEACH, AND ENCOURAGE THE VIRTUES.

Sometimes the only positive role model a student has in their life is their teacher. Be the light in the darkness.

Teresa Kwant

Recently I attended an awards assembly that acknowledged character trait award recipients along with academic awards. I love to support and encourage students by being there for their recognition. When a student received the "Caring" award, the audience clapped and cheered. His parents smiled from ear to ear.

But what happened next no doubt surprised everyone in the gym. The student presented his award to a classmate that he said needed it more than he did. The gym filled with an audible sigh, and the two students hugged.

I still don't know the reason behind this most generous gesture. Neither student explained. But the action clearly had a huge impact on them personally and on those who viewed the exchange.

On another day, I had my hands full of classroom supplies and was trying to negotiate a building entry door with my pinky finger. A student ran up and opened the door for me. I was so pleased that he had taken the time to notice that I needed help. Even more, he left his coveted recess to show courtesy. After I thanked him for his kindness,

I shot an email off to his teacher and his parents, thanking them for rearing such a thoughtful young man.

There's nothing more heartwarming than seeing students go the extra mile in caring about others. But those real-life stories also showcase something else: that students learn far more than academics in the classroom. The best education focuses also on developing students' hearts and their character. That's why, in establishing the Leman Academy of Excellence schools, we highlighted from the very beginning the understanding of six key virtues: caring, citizenship, perseverance, respect, responsibility, and trustworthiness. We believed these would empower our students to be kind, contributing members of their communities, and the best versions of themselves.[16]

What do we mean by these virtues? Here's a brief summary of each.[17]

Caring is being interested, concerned, and empathetic. Caring people express gratitude, kindness, compassion, forgiveness, and help others in need.

Citizenship means accepting the responsibility to contribute to the greater good of the community. Good citizens cooperate, respect authority, and obey rules and laws. They stay informed, vote, and are responsible, caring participants in school, local, state, and global communities.

Perseverance involves working hard to set and achieve personal goals, learning from failure, and following through with an undertaking to the end. People who persevere demonstrate commitment, pride, and a positive attitude to completing tasks.

Respect requires recognizing other people's feelings, opinions, or possessions. It is an attitude you display every day. When you treat others with respect, you accept differences, use good manners, and deal peacefully with anger, insults, and disagreements. Respectful people show high regard for authority, others, self, and country.

Responsibility requires taking control of your actions and obligations. It means taking ownership for something that is your fault, holding yourself accountable for your decisions and actions rather than pointing the finger at someone else. It means having a sense of duty to fulfill tasks with reliability, dependability, and commitment, and extends to self-discipline and work ethic. When you are responsible, you always do your best. Responsible people think before they act and consider the consequences.

Trustworthiness is being reliable, keeping your promises, and following through on your word. Trustworthy people are honest and have the courage to do the right thing.

It doesn't take a brain scientist to see how encouraging these character traits in the classroom will empower students toward success in all areas of life. They become people who do the right thing even when no one is looking. They treat others, no matter their differences, with respect. They complete their tasks and own up when they fall short. They do what they say they'll do. They never give up until the project is complete. They are caring and have a "we're all in this together" spirit. Such traits are part of pursuing a disciplined life.

Look down the road a few years. Who do you want your students to be? How do you want them to act? Then start with the end in mind, said Stephen R. Covey.[18] If you want your students to be kind, teach them to be kind. If you want them to be responsible, offer them responsibility and hold them accountable. If you want them to be respectful, teach and role-model respect in the classroom.

THE WAY OF THE TEACHER

Leonardo da Vinci once said, "Knowing is not enough; we must apply. Being willing is not enough; we must do." It all starts with you. Do you live out those virtues? Do your words match your actions? You light their way every day, and they *always* have their eyes on you.

Classroom Corner

* Of the six virtues we listed (Caring, Citizenship, Perseverance, Respect, Responsibility, Trustworthiness), which two would you pick as your highest goals in the classroom? Why?
* What virtue would you add to the list? Why? How might teaching and role-modeling that virtue impact your students' long-term character?

Teacher's Toolbelt

When students say or do something positive, comment on it. It might be a caring word or deed, perseverance on a project, or taking on increased responsibility. Make sure you specifically mention the associated virtue so students have the opportunity to view their positive choices in that light.

As you make such comments, students will start recognizing these attributes among classmates and express their appreciation too. The result? A classroom filled with caring individuals and a school community that bands together, making it a positive place to learn. Now that's a win-win environment for everyone.

FOCUS ON THE WHOLE CHILD.

The ability to think straight, some knowledge of the past, some vision of the future, some skill to do useful service, some urge to fit that service into the well-being of the community—these are the most vital things education must try to produce.

VIRGINIA GILDERSLEEVE

Have you ever had parents who believed their child wasn't learning enough in your class? If you have, it's not uncommon. Parents or guardians might request a more challenging curriculum or that their child skip a grade. Students may be reading a few grade levels ahead of their peers. Or perhaps math comes so naturally that the current grade's math is hardly a challenge. But are such steps actually the best thing for the child for the long run?

Education should be a partnership approach between the school and home. Your role is to help students reach their potential with the assistance of their parents and guardians. That means all parties need to be focused on the end goal. However, exactly what is that end goal? Parties may see it differently. That's why getting on the same page is so important.

We believe that students live up to the expectations teachers set for them. As educator Charlotte Mason said, "One of the secrets of power in dealing with our fellow-beings is to understand that human nature does that which it is expected to do and is that which it is expected to be." The shaping we do with our students should, at its core, be to help them reach their potential not only academically but socially, emotionally, and physically.

Mason's motto, "I am, I can, I ought, I will," encourages students to do what is right, to love what is lovely, and to take responsibility for their learning and behavior. It emphasizes self-discipline and the idea that right thinking leads to right acting. It focuses on character development and avoiding the easy way out.

In short, our job as educators is to help our scholars move toward what they should do and away from what they should not do. As Bob Talbert said, "Teaching kids to count is fine, but teaching kids what counts is best." More times than not, a child needs the opportunity to grow both vertical and horizontal roots to be well rounded and grounded.

If parents feel their child isn't learning enough in your class, point out gently that they are blessed indeed. Their child's academic prowess is rare. "How nice it must be to not have to worry about your child academically," you say. "Think of the family who struggles each night helping their child with homework, and everyone ends up in tears." Such words are a kind but subtle reality check.

Next, suggest activities to grow the child's roots horizontally. Possibilities include participating in a new sport, joining a chess club, or learning a musical instrument. The child could read more challenging materials at home in an area of interest or study a second language. She could take an art class or enroll in a martial arts class.

Education is all about teaching the whole child. If academics come easy, suggest an activity the student might be interested in but will have to work at. Team sports, for example, teach more than the skills required for that sport. They teach virtues such as teamwork and sportsmanship. They role model how to win graciously and how to handle defeat.

Assisting a child in reaching his potential is all about introducing opportunities that will help him grow broadly.

Classroom Corner

* How will you implement Mason's motto "I am, I can, I ought, I will" into your classroom?
* What good habits are you cultivating? What noble ideas are you shaping in your students that will assist them for a lifetime?

Teacher's Toolbelt

Want to encourage home partnership and get parents and guardians on the same page as you? Sending friendly emails out on a regular basis can assist in the flow of communication. Emails work well for general classroom news to ensure all parties have the same information. You can offer tips, emphasize concepts such as responsibility, accountability, age-appropriate decision-making, etc., that align with what students are learning in the classroom.

Following is an example of friendly tips that also teach concepts.

Tips for Organizing Kids in Transition

1. Brainstorm with your kids how they'd like to organize their incoming and outgoing schoolwork, backpack, shoes, jacket, and gym clothes. They might want to use color-coded folders, bins, or hooks. Allowing their choices to play out in practice will allow them to experience age-appropriate decision-making and real-life consequences.

2. Provide a consistent, sibling-free area in your home for their organizational system.

3. Teach your kids to start with the end in mind to get out the door to school on time. How long will it take them to get a shower? Get dressed? Eat breakfast? Gather any last-minute items? Let them do the math and set their alarms. Then roll with it. Showing up late to school one day and being a bit embarrassed is better than a long series of reminders to get up from Mom or Dad. Text me and let me know your game plan, and I'll happily roll with it.

4. Teach them how to pack their school lunch out of items you supply. This act puts the ball of responsibility squarely in the court of picky eaters, since they're packing their own lunches. It will also bring a reality check to those who demand on their way out the door, "Where's my lunch?" If they didn't pack it themselves, it's not there.

In all things, let real-life consequences for actions play out. It's for your own sanity and their learning potential.

CREATE AN INTENTIONAL CLASSROOM CULTURE.

It's not about what I can accomplish,
but what do I want to accomplish?
UNKNOWN

If someone walked in to your classroom right now to observe for half a day, what would he see? Would he answer yes or no to the following statements?

* Your classroom is a place of warmth, energy, learning, and encouragement.

* Your teaching space is organized and easy to navigate.

* Your seating arrangements allow for the advantages of small-group learning.

* Students are clearly used to classroom routines and follow them.

* You allow for movement and social interaction within your curriculum.

* You expect the best of your students.

* You do what you say you are going to do.

* You ask students to do something only once and expect them to follow through.

* Your students are respectful of your time and conversations with others.

* Your students feel free to ask you for help but also work well on their own.

* You actively listen with full attention and exhibit engagement with facial expressions and body language as students talk to you.

* Students listen attentively when other students talk and treat others respectfully.

* You handle negative behaviors with relational discipline, use the formula A + B = C, and let reality do the talking instead of you.

* When surprises happen, you are flexible, adaptable, and exhibit a sense of humor.

The answers to those questions would tell you a lot about your current classroom culture as others experience it. Where you are now might be your dream goal as a teacher, or you might have some areas to fine-tune. But here's the good news. Where you go from here is all up to you. You're in the driver's seat of your classroom car. You can keep aspects of the culture that you like and change aspects that you don't like.

Creating the classroom culture that you desire is all about intentionality. Being intentional means that you deliberately choose what you want to do and then purposefully take action steps to accomplish that intention. Teachers who create intentional classrooms:

* Know their why.

* Rehearse their why so they can voice it to their students, parents, other colleagues, staff, and administration.

* Practice their why with rubber-meets-the-road purpose.

* Refine their why as their skills and knowledge expand.

* Model their why in day-to-day life in the classroom.

* Live that why in all areas of life to be consistent in the message they give their students.

You must be the change you want to see in the classroom. That means you hold yourself to a higher standard of self-control. You choose to respond, thinking carefully of the consequences, rather than taking the temporarily easy route of reacting. You have high but manageable expectations of your students but even higher expectations of yourself.

Most of all, you take a long-term perspective. You are not simply responsible for a classroom of children for a school year. You're responsible for training adults-in-the-making and preparing them for life outside your classroom.

As you do so, remember that all behavior is purposive. Remove the purpose, and there's no need for the behavior. The power of understanding and positive expectations will change your conversations for the good. Focus on winning your students' cooperation. Offer to listen, but don't force communication. Exercise patience…and wait. Be your student's advocate and lifeline when they need it. However, don't try to solve their dilemmas. Oftentimes they already know the answer. They just need you to listen as they process.

Your words and actions have the ability to break your students' spirits or the opportunity to support, encourage, and empower them. Why not create the classroom environment that you'd be happy to call "home"? Today's a great day to start. As performance coach Michael Hyatt says, "The busier you are, the more intentional you must be."

Classroom Corner

* What kind of classroom environment do you want to create? Write down your goals in a concise statement you can look at every day as a reminder.

* Anne Frank said, "Everyone has inside them a piece of good news. The good news is you don't know how great you can be! How much you can love! What you can accomplish! And what your potential is." How might this quote encourage you to view a troublesome student with long-range perspective?

Teacher's Toolbelt

Younger kids like to choose out of a treasure chest. It's the only way I got my own children to the dentist. They knew that they could pick from the dentist's treasure chest and take home a trinket after their appointments.

Teachers can spend a lot of money keeping their classroom treasure chest filled with prizes to encourage students. How can you better manage that without spending so much money? The reality is that our students don't need things. You can save your money and try a little Vitamin E instead. Encouragement is what students crave. Recognizing their hard work and accomplishments will pay off more than the latest little toy.

Every once in a while it's fun to do something special for your class. And not because they earned it but because you care about them and want to do something nice. For example, an ice-pop party on a warm day can be a sweet, inexpensive treat.

However, move away from giving weekly physical rewards. Instead, use your words of encouragement to the group or handwritten notes that uniquely acknowledge each of your students. Leave a sticky note on their cubby, write a message in Expo marker on their desks, and watch their faces light up. Young kids especially want to be loved by you. What a relief that you can do that all day, every day, and it never has to cost you a dime.

PRINCIPLE #37

WELCOME PARTNERS WITH OPPORTUNITIES AND A ROADMAP.

TEACH...
Together
Everyone
ACHieves more.
STEPHANIE SMOLEN

Ask teachers how they feel about volunteers in the classroom and you'll get a wide range of responses.

* "The more, the merrier. I can always use an extra hand."

* "It takes a lot of time to line things up. I don't have that kind of time."

* "I'd rather do things myself because I know they'll get done the right way."

* "Volunteers always bring new perspective and life lessons."

* "My school encourages volunteers. But in the past, I've found that parents only come in to watch me teach and help their own child."

If you have concerns about volunteers in the classroom, we get it. Teaching in front of other adults instead of only you and your students can change the classroom dynamic. Your hesitancy to involve volunteers is understandable, especially when setting up tasks for them to do can also be time-consuming.

Perhaps it's time to try something new. The following strategies will help you get over your hesitancy and take advantage of this resource that will buy you time and enrich your class with new experiences. Instead of being nervous about volunteers, approach them with the positive assumption that they have the best of intentions.

No, we're not naive enough to think that some parents don't have a hidden agenda for wanting to get in to your classroom. However, the majority truly do want to help. They sometimes don't know how and are a little awkward and shy. That's why they gravitate to their own child, the one they know. They need to know that it's not only okay but expected and appreciated to roam the room helping as many children as possible.

I strongly encourage you to have an organized system in place for volunteers. Make it simple. As Albert Einstein said, "If you can't explain it simply, you don't understand it yourself." Clearly explain to volunteers that you greatly appreciate their assistance with specific tasks. Such tasks can be anything from photocopying to assisting students with a science experiment or driving on a field trip.

Communicate to parents how to sign up to volunteer so you know who is coming and their arrival time. State that working alongside other people's children requires confidentiality. Finally, explain your organizational system and where to find materials and instructions for their tasks as they enter the classroom.

Before volunteers arrive, prep a bin, file folder, or organized system with the items you want them to do and specific directions. This minimizes classroom distractions. When parents enter your room, you don't have to stop your lesson. A smile and a nod of acknowledgment will do. Leave a little note in the bin, thanking them for sharing their time in supporting your classroom. At a natural break in your instruction, you can then greet the volunteers and check in to see if they have any questions.

You'll get to know your parents and their strengths as they volunteer. Some love working one-on-one or in small groups with kids. Others prefer tasks that don't involve direct contact with students because they're introspective and a bit uncomfortable with people interaction. Still others can pull off classroom fun and parties like they're born to organize and celebrate. Others love to talk about their vocations as motivational guest speakers or read stories or chapters of books to the class over lunch. You need all types in your classroom.

Many hands make light work, so if parents want to come help, embrace them. Use this also as a time to foster those parent-teacher relationships. Remember, teaching is all about the 3Rs: Relationship, Relationship, Relationship.

Classroom Corner

* In what areas could you most use volunteers?
* How might you incorporate those volunteers to save you time, to provide interesting information that your class can't get out of textbooks, and to expand your students' horizons and perspectives? Why not try one of those ideas this month?

Teacher's Toolbelt

Some parents want to volunteer, but their career or other circumstances keeps them from being available during the school day. Here are a few ways they can contribute.

* Have a "Volunteer Night" in your classroom. Give parents a room tour and directions on what to do. They will feel more confident knowing the location of supplies and what to start on when they arrive.

* Survey parents via email to find areas they're most comfortable helping with and assign projects accordingly to those who are interested in assisting.

* Offer projects that can be done at home, such as cutting or organizing pieces for an art project.

* Encourage them to run a station during your fall evening celebration.

* Find areas around your room that need a little "umph." Parents can be awesome for recreating a bulletin board or freshening up a space in the few minutes after school where you're catching up on schoolwork.

* Ask some parents to be library parents. Give them a list of topics you're teaching in upcoming weeks and ask if they'd be willing to pick up some library books for the class. Provide a library bag so you can keep the books organized and make the exchange between parent and teacher an easy one.

When volunteers assist, don't forget to have the class greet and thank them by name. Such an action models respect and appreciation for their service. Throughout the year, celebrate volunteers, including having students sign thank you cards. Consider a small gift of appreciation at the end of the year. A little bit of thanks goes a long way to develop relationships.

TAP INTO THE GRANDPARENT TREASURE TROVE.

Grandparents, like heroes, are as necessary
to a child's growth as vitamins.
JOYCE ALLSTON

Let me ask you, how many people had your back as a kid? Loved you as you were? Believed in you despite evidence to the contrary?

We have asked people that question thousands of times. Know what the answer is? The average is between one and two. Most people don't say, "Well, I had 15." If you can say that, consider yourself rare and blessed indeed. Then go out and do the same thing for one or more kids where such support could make all the difference in their current circumstances and life choices.

Many grandparents have built-in abilities to love children the way they are, with all their flaws, missteps, and phenomenal learning potential. That unconditional love is another layer of foundation of security for each of those children. Grandparents are not only family but can become friends who grow with the children through all their stages and discoveries.

Yes, grandparents are one step removed from parents, but it's a healthy step in our view. As I always say, "The nicest thing about being a grandparent is that we can just love them. After they are with us for an evening or weekend, we give them back." And then in true grandparent fashion we also take a good, long nap to recover from all that youthful energy and enthusiasm.

Healthy, involved grandparents are an integral part of a child's life. This is especially true for children whose parents have dual time-consuming careers, and single parents who don't have time to brush their teeth before the next demand hits. Teachers miss a great opportunity by not including the treasure trove of grandparents in their communications and classroom activities.

Grandparents have myriad life experiences and subsequent perspective to share. They also often love to volunteer in the classroom. Their former careers, skills, and specialties make them very handy for classroom enrichment activities because they grew up in eras where they sometimes had to make do if they didn't have what they needed.

Take the 81-year-old grandma who was visiting her grandchild's classroom when the art teacher suddenly became ill. The first graders had time for an art session, but no project to do. That grandma stepped right up to the plate. She showed those fascinated first graders how to cut one-of-a-kind snowflakes out of plain white photocopy paper. She whipped the spool of white thread she always had in her voluminous handbag to create loops so the children could hang their very own snowflakes in their classroom window.

After that, the impressed art teacher made it a yearly project and used it to decorate her art room windows during the month of January. That resourceful grandma returned every year for eight years to aid the classroom in the project. It was a hit all 'round. Now that's ingenuity, and grandparents have plenty of it. So why not tap into it for classroom fun and to give you the brain break you need and deserve during art time or any time?

Or take the 90-year-old grandpa who had been a soldier in two wars and then a history teacher. Even the cool high-school kids would gather like little ducklings around Papa Duck in the cafeteria every Friday when he shared stories of his experiences.

It's true today's grandparents don't always live in the same state as their grandkids. Distance and physical issues may not make it easy to enter the classroom. But there are plenty of things they can do. They can write encouraging notes, record videos of life experiences, or share stories of different time periods and locales. The sky's the limit with some brainstorming.

Most of all, they can freely love their grandchildren and their peers. What a joy it is to see grandparents we know scoop up kids who don't have family in the classroom and enfold them into their little circle on Grandparents' Day. With all the love, time, and life wisdom they have to share, why not take advantage of such a treasure trove for yours and your students' benefit?

Classroom Corner

* How might grandparents assist you in your to-do list for this week? Why not send out an email or make a few calls?

* Why not ask an enterprising and organized grandparent if he or she would be willing to coordinate a "Grandparent Help Station" or something similar? Sure, it would take a half hour or so after school or over lunch one day to explain what you're looking for at first. But it's a small price to pay for a streamlined network of assistance the rest of the school year.

Teacher's Toolbelt

The classroom is enriched every time students see multi-generations enter its door. That action sends a message that those inside are cared for by many. Grandparents can help serve lunch, read to a reluctant reader, or work with a small group in math.

They could also be a good buddy at a "Buddy Bench." At Leman Academy of Excellence, each playground area has a bench designed especially for students of all ages to communicate they need a friend. It always brings me joy to see a student courageously choose to sit on the bench, and then, moments later, be surrounded by other students willing to step in and help. Many grandparents would be thrilled to also fulfill that buddy role.

If your school doesn't host an annual Grandparents' Day, we'd highly recommend you spearhead that endeavor. Grandparents come for the morning, see the classrooms, do an art project alongside their grandchild, and learn more about the school. Our annual Grandparents' Day runs simultaneously with our school's book fair. Grandparents love to buy books for their grandkids and see their classroom. It's a win-win for all.

DON'T FORGET
THE FUN FACTOR.

Two things reduce prejudice: education and laughter.
LAURENCE J. PETER

When I was a kid, I thought school was the most boring place on earth. No wonder I escaped it as much as I could, army-crawling out of a lecture to the tune of my classmates' laughter when the teacher's back was turned. That teacher's face turned an apoplectic red because he had no idea what was going on. He believed the class was laughing at *him*, instead of at little Kevin Leman, who resembled an earthworm in spring.

Think about this perspective for a minute. School to me was so boring that waiting for the fish to bite in a creek in upstate New York was far more exciting. *Ouch.*

You see, when school isn't FUN, no one wants to be there. Teachers or students. But if you up the Fun Factor, you can turn around their attitudes swiftly. Let me ask you, if you were a student, which options would you choose in the following two scenarios?

SCENARIO #1: Your science curriculum focuses on reptiles: their environment, food, actions, and the differences between males and females.

Ways to Learn

Option #1: Read about Russian tortoises in a textbook. Answer the questions at the end of each chapter as a mini-quiz.

Option #2: Watch a science film or YouTube video about Russian tortoises. Write a double-spaced page about what you learned.

Option #3: Have an opportunity to babysit a pair of Russian tortoises in your classroom. The owner of the reptiles introduces you to them and tells you what he's learned about them over 14 years. For a week you get to watch as they move about their habitat, dig and burrow, eat, and sleep. You learn first-hand what foods they need to keep them healthy, what illnesses they are susceptible to, and how to know if a tortoise is healthy or sick. You learn how to hold and support them properly. You see their biological differences in their tail structure since one is female and one is male.

Each day a different group of students is responsible to care for those tortoises. The students provide fresh food and water. They keep track of what the reptiles eat and drink on a chart and clean their habitat. The group decides themselves how to divvy up the tasks of an agreed-upon checklist. Some come to school 15 minutes early, some stay after school, and others forfeit their brain break or recess time to do so.

SCENARIO #2: The class is learning Spanish as a second language.

Ways to Learn

Option #1: Learn Spanish basics, including how to count and use correct grammar, from a textbook. Take mini-evaluations at each chapter's end and a final written test.

Option #2: Listen to video lectures and repeat Spanish phrases after the facilitator.

Option #3: Spanish speakers visit class for mini-sessions two days a week. They teach you how to count and communicate basic phrases such as, "Hi, I'm (your name)," "Thank you," and "I'd like to find/buy X." They bring Hispanic foods for you to try, if there's no one in your class with dietary issues. For your test, you dialogue one-on-one with a Spanish speaker in a conversation real people might have. That person laughs with you when you make mistakes, and you get to try again until you perfect that word or phrase.

All options get the job done of learning about tortoises and Spanish language basics. But, hands down, we're confident you'd pick Option #3 in both scenarios. Why? Because they're not boring. They're fun!

If you are the sage on the stage who lectures, reads off slides, or pops in a video, students are likely to disengage and lack motivation. Think of their state as the haze you feel prior to having your coffee, tea, or green juice for the day. But get those students up and moving, collaborating, and creatively learning in an exciting environment, and you'll have invigorated students. They don't have to work hard to learn, and you don't have to work hard to teach them. They're intrigued, so they learn naturally.

Let the Fun Factor reign.

Classroom Corner

* Before you teach a concept, ask yourself, *How might I do this differently? Make it more exciting?* We know you can come up with some fun variations.

* Remember, when it's fun for your students, it's also fun for you. If you find yourself bored by the same old curriculum, make a

change. Teach that required curriculum in a fresh way that will energize you too.

Teacher's Toolbelt

We already talked about 7 Essential Vitamins in Principle #33. Now we'd like to add one more: *Vitamin L = Laughter.* Laughter is an essential ingredient to a well-rounded child. It's like water to a growing plant. The classroom that laughs *together* (note: not *at* each other, which is hurtful and erects barriers) builds classroom community and solves disputes faster than any other method.

Don't let a day pass by without the Fun Factor and Laughter as part of that. As a byproduct, it'll lessen your stress and make you more light-hearted. Here are a few ideas to try.

* Greet each student at the door with a good morning smile.

* Create a unique handshake or greeting to exchange with each student.

* Notice small things, like the first dandelion when warm weather hits. Tell your class, "Do you know today is the first day of spring? Right outside our window, there's a sign of it. If you spot it, call it out. Let's all move to the window...."

* Create hands-on, engaging lessons. If you're learning about plants, place plants all over your classroom. Bring the outdoors inside as much as possible.

Charlotte Mason said, "An observant child should be put in the way of things worth observing." Look around your room. What could you add to pique curiosity and allow for more observation, discovery, and wonder?

GREAT TEACHERS MAKE GREAT STUDENTS.

If you look behind every exceptional person,
there is an exceptional teacher.
STEPHEN HAWKING

Did you know that you have a leading role in each of your students' life stories? That's because you matter far more than you think. When you focus on developing the whole child and a relationship with that unique child, you are helping to develop the next generation of thinkers and doers. As Abraham Lincoln said, "The best way to predict the future is to create it." And you, Teacher, are doing that every single day. Talk about a valiant career.

You're the teacher who helped a frustrated first-grader learn how to tie his shoes. You comforted a third-grader who cried a river of tears because someone said she was stupid. After school, you sat beside her as she wrestled through an assignment on her own.

When a fifth-grader didn't contribute to a group, you let him make that choice. The group did their presentation, and he had nothing to present. A+B=C reigned. He worked for a week, forfeiting his brain breaks, to present a new topic all by himself to the class. You heard him mutter, "That was dumb. I'll never do that again." As soon as the next group project arrived, he jumped into the action.

You cheered on an eighth-grader who organized a marathon to raise money for her mom's leukemia treatment. That day you donned your athletic shoes and ran to support her and the cause. Seeing the joy and admiration on her face at the end of the road was worth all the sweat and effort.

Such moves were important not only then but for those students' futures. Now that first-grader is a life coach. That third-grader is teaching reluctant readers. That fifth-grader took over his dad's business and is growing it like wildfire. That eighth-grader is pursuing a business degree. Don't you think that you, Teach, had a little bit to do with each of those plans?

We believe wholeheartedly that "The purpose of education is not to fill the minds of students with facts…It is to teach them to think… and always to think for themselves," as Robert M. Hutchins said. Yes, students may get there by themselves. But they might get there a whole lot faster with assistance from great teachers.

In this book, we've focused on four key areas: A Teacher's Mindset, Classroom Strategies, Student Relations, and Goals and Perspective. No book could say everything you need to know about teaching. This is the tip of the iceberg. But let's quickly review what we've learned thus far, shall we?

First, *having the right mindset is critical to stepping confidently into the classroom and finding fulfillment in your work even when things don't go as planned.* You are the authority and the change-maker. Knowing your strengths, weaknesses, and hot buttons helps you deal with students and parents who might be very like you or very different from you.

When you cultivate good habits, including organization and goal-setting, everything will run better. When you are honest about what you know and don't know, seek help when you need it, and are open to new ideas, teaching will never be boring. Respond rather than react, and you won't suffer open-mouth-insert-foot syndrome. Set yourself up for a great year with students and their parents through the power of positivity and staying flexible and adaptable.

Second, *forming your classroom strategies and staying the course is paramount to a successful school year*. Start off on the right foot with the strategies we've suggested, and you'll be light years ahead of your peers. Use technology intentionally and sparingly. Highlight small-group instruction and interaction for energetic, intriguing learning.

If you want your students to listen, whisper. Give them the opportunity to be responsible and hold them accountable. Expect the best. When you don't get that best, address the root cause. Get ahead of the game on parent-teacher conference expectations. Treat teaching like the contact sport it is.

Third, *realize that a relationship with your students is your highest calling*. Don't treat them the same because they aren't the same. Understand what kids want most and fear most. Seek out hurting kids and loners. Address the unique child, not the label.

Enter the tumultuous teen zone with knowledge and empathy. If you want your students to talk, shut up and listen. Never, ever do for a child what she should do for herself. Yes, they will make missteps. When you know it's one of those days, offer them grace…like you'd want to receive.

Fourth, *remember to stick to your goals and exercise long-range perspective*. View your students as lifelong learners and focus on developing the whole child. Provide the 7+1 Essential Vitamins, and model, teach, and encourage the virtues. Address the *why* to turn behavior around. Intentionally create the kind of classroom culture that you'd want to be a part of. Welcome volunteers of all ages with a roadmap. Most of all, don't forget the fun.

Do these things, and students will be saying years down the road, "Remember Ms. X? And when she did X? She made me feel smart, loved, and not alone in this world. She believed in me. Without her, I wouldn't be doing what I'm doing today."

THE WAY OF THE TEACHER

Classroom Corner

* Which of the four areas remains your greatest challenge? Hone in on one aspect this week. Make notes about your progress and reread them for encouragement.

* Guy Kawasaki said, "If you have to put someone on a pedestal, put teachers. They are society's heroes." When have you been a champion or role model for a student? Reflect on one of those times and what it taught you.

Teacher's Toolbelt

We've given you a wealth of toolbelt ideas in this book. We know you haven't had time to try them all. Why not pick one of your favorites and do it today?

WHAT KIND OF TEACHER ARE YOU?

What You Need Most

TEACHER #1

1. Know you are not alone. You're standing in a massive field of teachers who, like you, need empathy (and, yes, some sympathy) and are craving assistance but are reticent to ask for it. All teachers get a little overwhelmed sometimes. It's what they decide to do with that feeling that makes the difference between staying overwhelmed and getting proactive in their search for assistance.

2. Take a few hours of mini-holiday on an evening or weekend to write down your areas of personal strength and professional strength. For example:

* I'm pretty creative on a limited budget.
* I'm really good at teaching math using everyday objects so problems make sense to my students.

Do yourself a huge favor. Post that list where you can see it first thing in the morning. It will give you a positive start to each classroom day.

3. Identify one specific area of weakness. Brainstorm realistic, actionable ways to strengthen that weakness. For example:

* *Weakness:* I'm disorganized, so I waste time locating class materials.
* *Brainstorms:* Buy plastic, stackable bins, one for each subject, that I can color-code and label. Organize the next day's materials for each subject at the end of each school day.

See, look at you go! You've bought yourself an evening free of "I should be doing something about that" guilt and the kind of morning relief that no antacid could provide. Your whole day will go better with that approach.

4. Ask another teacher known for her positive attitude to take an after-school break with you. Offer to bring the sandwiches. Start with a simple question. "Could I ask your opinion about something? I'd really appreciate your help...." Most people, when asked for advice in such a nice way with the perk of food, would be happy to join you for a friendly conversation.

Examples of starter questions might be:

* "Have you ever had a parent insist their child should get all As? If so, what did you do?"
* "A child in my class always ends up the center of attention because he's so animated and distracting. But I don't want to squash his enthusiasm, either. How would you handle that situation?"

Not only will you get fresh ideas, but such an exchange may prompt the two of you to invite others to join. If you keep the focus on problem-solving and limit the session to 20 minutes once a month, most teachers would love to participate in such healthy networking.

5. Be proactive with administration. Ask, "I'd love to refine my teaching skills. Is it possible for me to observe some masterful teachers in this school? Or to attend outside workshops or classes?" Healthy administrators who are passionate about education would welcome such an approach and be happy to provide options.

TEACHER #2

1. Know that what you do every day not only matters, but matters greatly in the lives of your students now and will impact their futures.

2. Realize that being detailed is a good thing, but not everyone will be as detail-oriented as you are. Schools need various skills to make the teaching world go 'round. Sometimes minor incidents are just…minor. Each of us needs to give and receive grace sometimes.

3. Start a personal "Happy Things" journal, where you can list your small and large achievements every day and how they make you feel. Skimming the entries once a week will help meet your need for recognition and compliments. It also provides a healthy perspective that good things are happening overall in your classroom and at school, even when you have an occasional bad day.

   Amidst the clamor of everything going on at school, it would be easy to focus on solving problems, both large and small, as they arise. However, it's important to remember that *your needs* are also important. Reflecting on your journal and its repeated themes will also provide clues to your unmet needs. At what moments were you happiest and most fulfilled? How might you engineer more of those moments?

4. Understand that people won't always be happy with you. In fact, there are some people who are never happy, and you can never do enough to keep them happy. You know exactly what we're talking about. But there's a long-term lesson here. I've always said, "An unhappy person is a healthy person." No one should get their way all the time. It's not realistic, nor is it healthy.

Your role isn't to make parents and grandparents happy with you all the time. It's to partner with the home to the best of your ability in educating the whole child. Sometimes that means holding the line on what you know is the right thing to do and letting the temporary unhappiness reign for the greater long-term good.

Reflecting on your journal will also provide clues as to why others' approval and making them happy is so important to you. Understanding the *why* will assist you in bringing a more holistic perspective to events and conversations.

5. Use your penchant for comparison to liven up and brighten the school atmosphere by motivating healthy, positive competition. Suggest to administration that they introduce a "Teacher for the Week Award," where teachers are encouraged to be caught doing something good. You might want to introduce a weekly "Spirit of the Class Award" for your students to boost morale and encourage caring acts.

TEACHER #3

1. We applaud your keen attention to organization and details in providing structure and a clear game plan for your classroom. You are truly one in a million, and such skills are prized at schools.

2. Instead of viewing new ideas as trying to fix something that's not broken, think of them as adding to what is already working. Since respect for structure and your time is at the top of your list of desirable traits, it's no surprise you aren't crazy about rambling meetings or idea workshops. Simply changing how you view such an exchange can transform the way you approach those meetings. Sure, you'd rather be tackling your to-do list or grading tests. However, your smile and attention in the moment will say mountains to your colleagues about your professionalism and team spirit.

   When you leave that meeting, what you do with those ideas is up to you. You can try an idea or two or evaluate their worth and figuratively toss them out your classroom window. But why not do yourself a favor and give yourself the benefits of a fresh wind every once in a while?

3. Start a "Someday" file of ideas and try one new idea once a week for six weeks. You might be surprised how the break in routine introduces some excitement and fun you haven't felt in years.

4. Reflect on this question: "Why do I resist new ideas and forming relationships?" Have you had negative experiences with other teachers and administrators? Did you grow up as an only child, who had to do things on her own so you got used to doing things that way? Or as a firstborn, who had to blaze a trail for her siblings to follow under parental eagle eyes?

The poet John said it well: "No man [or woman] is an island entire of itself."[19] Working with others can be frustrating, especially if they aren't as structured and goal-oriented as you are. You've got a good thing going in the classroom. Other teachers, especially first-years, can learn a lot from you. Why not look for openings to contribute your wealth of knowledge and experience to another teacher or two? Don't keep your ideas to yourself. They're too good not to share.

5. Ask administration if they'd be willing for you to assist with gathering concerns, making an easy-to-follow agenda, and keeping discussions on track during teacher meetings. You could help plan meetings at least a week in advance and provide the agenda to teachers a couple of days before the meeting. Why not put your organizational skills and desire for routine to use in lessening your frustration and benefitting the entire school community?

TEACHER #4

1. Know how much students, parents, grandparents, administrators, and your colleagues need teachers like you to develop an invigorating, positive learning environment.

2. Realize how rare masterful teachers like you are. It's relatively easy to follow a set plan. It's harder to have confidence and skills in your teaching style and methods. And it's harder yet to be able to adapt those methods based on the makeup of your class each year.

    You are taking education to a whole 'nother level, so pat yourself on the back. You'll likely have to do it yourself. Others may think you walk on water so much that you don't need encouragement or affirmation.

    If and when you find someone who truly understands how much of a treasure you are, accept the compliment with a big smile. You deserve it…and more.

3. To be able to mentor and share your masterful skills, but in a regular, controlled fashion.

    Instead of getting bombarded by individual teachers, why not ask administration if you could do several half-hour workshops each school year on specific topics of importance to teachers? That would give you time to prepare and allow you to spread your positive influence without taking your daily focus off your own classroom. The bonus is that, after three or four years, you'll have ready-to-go workshops you could repeat for teacher training.

    If you are still getting requests from teachers, why not schedule a half-hour session once a month after school and invite any teachers who want to come? Clarify the purpose of the meeting up front: a time to mutually problem-solve and discuss issues of importance to teachers. Any situations must be presented as theoretical, without names or details that could identify persons given. That will assist in encouraging healthy dialogue and discouraging gossip.

4. Set some parameters on your open-door policy. Perhaps your door is open for the first or last 15 minutes of your lunch period. Or it's open on Tuesdays and Thursdays, but closed on Monday, Wednesday, and Friday. You deserve a break.

5. Realize that, while you walk on water, you'll sink if your boat is overloaded with tasks and mentorship. You also need assistance and support. If school administrators are smart and healthy, they will welcome your ideas to keep your work in the classroom and the clamoring for mentorship to a balance you're comfortable with.

THE FINAL WORD

Education is not the filling of a pail, but the lighting of a fire.
WILLIAM BUTLER YEATS

Teachers have the rarest of opportunities: to influence the world for good every single day.

However, teaching is not for everyone. It's certainly not for the faint of heart. It takes great stamina, a heart for children, and a passion for your content. If you have that, you are headed in the right direction, no matter whether you are a newbie teacher, a veteran of many years, or anywhere in the middle.

Like with any practice, teaching takes time to master, along with a lot of trial and error. For those of you who are new to teaching, recognize that the first year can be challenging. You may wonder whether the job is for you or you are any good at it. But never fear. Teachers in their second year feel overwhelmingly more confident with their content and craft. Each year gets better and better. Ask any veteran teacher.

Perseverance, patience, and, yes, a good sense of humor, are keys to refining your craft and striving for excellence. Better yet, the lifelong learning potential is never over with plenty of fresh ideas, such as the ones we've shared, and a spirit of adventure. If you're reading this book, you've already embraced this amazing profession. You desire to be a difference maker, to educate rising leaders of tomorrow who will make their own positive imprint on the world.

So here's our guarantee: if you give teaching your very best effort, the rewards will be countless. Your legacy will live on in the hearts, minds, and lives of your students. You'll have no regrets that you didn't do all you could to make this world a better place.

As Lyndon B. Johnson sagely stated, "At the desk where I sit, I have learned one great truth…. The answer for all the problems of the world…comes to a single word. That word is *education*."

A STUDENT'S 10 COMMANDMENTS TO TEACHERS

1. Let me spread my wings and try to fly, but keep me from falling too fast.
2. Don't tell me what to do. Allow me to figure things out on my own.
3. Expect the best of me, trust me, and believe in me. Deep down I really want to please you. You are far more important to me than you could ever know.
4. Give me another chance when I mess up. Sometimes I need to learn the hard way, but I will learn from my mistakes.
5. Talk *with* me instead of *at* me, and listen first…always.
6. Realize I'm doing the best I can in a tough, intense world.
7. Provide unchanging rules I can count on to keep me safe.
8. Accept me for who I am now, and encourage me in who I am becoming.
9. Tell me when I do wrong, but don't judge me. Never criticize me. It hurts too deeply.
10. Admit when you blow it, say you're sorry, and you'll have my loyalty and gratitude forever.

NOTES

1   Astrid Nehlig, "The neorprotective effects of cocoa flavanol and its influence on cognitive performance," BJCP, Feb. 5, 2013, doi: 10.1111/j.1365-2125.2012.04378.x in NLM, https://www.ncbi.nlm.nih.gov/pmc/articles/PMC3575938/.

2   Jon Gordon, "Jon Gordon's Post," Linkedin, https://www.linkedin.com/posts/jongordonenergy_being-positive-doesnt-just-make-you-better-activity.

3   Jon Gordon, "The 7 Steps" in "The Power of a Positive You," https://jongordon.com/wp-content/uploads/2023/03/Power_of_Positive_You_PDF.pdf.

4   Sean Blackmer, "Movement in The Classroom," *TEACH Magazine,* Jan. 7, 2024, https://teachmag.com/archives/10678.

5   WOHM, "The Impact of Technology on Child Development: The Pros and Cons," Feb. 8, 2023, https://wohum.org/the-impact-of-technology-on-child-development-the-pros-and-cons/.

6   Jon Johnson, "Negative effects of technology: What to know," *Medical News Today,* Apr. 5, 2023, https://www.medicalnewstoday.com/articles/negative-effects-of-technology.

7   WOHM, "The Impact of Technology on Child Development: The Pros and Cons."

8   CDC, "Screen Time vs. Lean Time," Division of Nutrition, Physical Activity, and Obesity, CDC, Jan. 29, 2018, https://www.cdc.gov/nccdphp/dnpao/multimedia/infographics/getmoving.html.

9   Alyson Klein, "1,500 Decisions a Day (At Least!O): How Teachers Cope With a Dizzying Array of Questions," Dec. 6, 2021, *Education Week,* https://www.edweek.org/teaching-learning/1-500-decisions-a-day-at-least-how-teachers-cope-with-a-dizzying-array-of-questions/2021/12.

10   Larry Shaffer, "You really can learn as much from failure as you do success," *Fast Company,* Jun. 19, 2022, https://www.fastcompany.com/90761446/you-really-can-learn-as-much-from-failure-as-you-do-success#.

11   NIMH, "Eating Disorders," National Institute for Mental Health, https://www.nimh.nih.gov/health/statistics/eating-disorders.

12   Amanda Morin, "Teaching with empathy: Why it's important," Understood.org, https://www.understood.org/articles/teaching-with-empathy-why-its-important.

13   Source unknown.

14   Pedagogy4change.org, "Great Pedagogical Thinkers: James P. Comer."

15   Julia Cook, *Ricky Sticky Fingers,* National Center for Youth Issues, August 28, 2012, https://www.amazon.com/Ricky-Sticky-Fingers-Julia-Cook/dp/1937870081.

16   Leman Academy of Excellence, "Education for the Mind and Heart," https://lemanacademy.com/discover-leman-academy/our-approach/our-virtues/.

17   Ibid.

18   Stephen R. Covey, *The 7 Habits of Highly Effective People* (London, UK: Simon & Schuster, 2013), cover. His exact phrase was "Begin with the end in mind."

19   John Donne, "No Man Is An Island," *Meditation XVII: Devotions upon Emergent Occasions,* https://web.cs.dal.ca/~johnston/poetry/island.html.

ABOUT DR. KEVIN LEMAN

An internationally known psychologist, radio and television personality, educator, speaker, and humorist, Dr. Kevin Leman has taught and entertained audiences worldwide with his wit and commonsense psychology.

The *New York Times* bestselling and award-winning author of over 70 books, including *The Birth Order Book, Have a New Kid by Friday, Sheet Music, Making Children Mind without Losing Yours, Parenting the Powerful Child, Be the Dad She Needs You to Be, The Way of the Shepherd, 8 Secrets to Raising Successful Kids, 7 Things He'll Never Tell You but You Need to Know, Why Kids Misbehave,* and *Planet Middle School,* Dr. Leman has made thousands of house calls through radio and television programs, including *FOX & Friends*, Hallmark Channel's *Home & Family, The View*, FOX's *The Morning Show, Today*, Dr. Bill Bennett's *Morning in America, The List, Today, Oprah, The 700 Club*, CBS's *The Early Show*, CNN, and *Focus on the Family*.

Dr. Leman has served as a contributing family psychologist to *Good Morning America*. He frequently speaks to schools, CEO groups, businesses—including Fortune 500 companies and others such as YPO, Million Dollar Round Table, and Top of the Table—and civic and church organizations. A practicing psychologist for over 40 years, Dr. Kevin Leman has helped millions of adults understand the dynamics of healthy relationships.

His professional affiliations include the American Psychological Association and the North American Society of Adlerian Psychology. He received the Distinguished Alumnus Award (1993) and an honorary Doctor of Humane Letters degree (2010) from North Park University, and a bachelor's degree in psychology, his master's and doctorate degrees, as well as the Alumni Achievement Award (2003)—the highest award they can give one of their own—from the University of Arizona. Dr. Leman is the founder of Leman Academy of Excellence (www.lemanacademy.com).

Originally from Williamsville, New York, Dr. Leman and his wife, Sande, live in Tucson, Arizona. They have five children and four grandchildren.

If you're looking for an entertaining speaker for your event or fund-raiser, please contact:

> Dr. Kevin Leman
> PO Box 35370
> Tucson, Arizona 85740
> Phone: (520) 797-3830
> www.birthorderguy.com

Follow Dr. Kevin Leman on Facebook (Facebook.com/DrKevinLeman) and on X (@DrKevinLeman). Check out the free podcasts at birthorderguy.com/podcast.

For "Dr. Kevin Leman" resources on marriage, parenting, family, and many other topics: amazon.com.

For more about Leman Academy of Excellence: lemanacademy.com.

ABOUT KRISTIN LEMAN O'REILLY

Kristin Leman O'Reilly began her educational journey nearly three decades ago. She holds an M.A. in Teaching, a B.A. in Elementary Education, and a B.A. in Psychology. She has taught in both private and charter schools, holding various leadership roles as Director of Curriculum and Instruction, Curriculum Coordinator, Professional Development Administrator, and Vice Principal.

Passionate about mentoring teachers and training them to be life-long learners to inspire the next generation of leaders, Kristin created a Teacher Recognition Program to honor teachers and shower them with the appreciation they deserve. She annually trained nearly 400 incoming and resident teachers, as well as supporting them throughout the year with ongoing Professional Development workshops.

Kristin is also coauthor with Dr. Kevin Leman of *Be a Great Teacher by Friday: 5 Winning Plays to Spark World-Changing Potential* (BroadStreet, 2025). She, her husband, Dennis, and children, Conner and Adeline, reside in Tucson, Arizona.

Follow her at Facebook.com/KristinLemanOReilly and on Instagram.com/KristinLemanOReilly.

For "Kristin Leman O'Reilly" resources: amazon.com.